How to Lead Work Teams: Facilitation Skills

How to Lead Work Teams: Facilitation Skills

Fran Rees

San Diego • Toronto • Amsterdam • Sydney

Copyright © 1991 by Pfeiffer & Company
ISBN: 0-88390-056-4
Library of Congress Catalog Card Number: 91-6561
Printed in the United States of America

Rees, Fran.
   How to lead work teams : facilitation skills / Fran Rees.
      p.   cm.
   Includes bibliographical references and index.
   ISBN 0-88390-056-4
   1. Work groups—Management.   I. Title.
HD66.R394   1991
658.4 ′ 03—dc20

Cover Design/Art/Page Composition:
Kris Kircher

Pfeiffer & Company
8517 Production Avenue
San Diego, California 92121
Phone (619) 578-5900
FAX (619) 578-2042

Contents

Introduction

Many American companies are striving to increase the involvement of employees in what was once the domain of management. They are increasingly aware that employees' ideas and opinions can help solve critical organization problems. Several factors are influencing this shift toward more employee participation:

- Given the complexity of jobs and information, it is nearly impossible for managers to make all the decisions. They have a growing awareness that decisions should be made by those with the best information. In many cases, the person closest to the job is the one who should decide.
- The focus on quality and customer satisfaction has riveted attention on the importance of each employee's work.
- The shift from a homogeneous to a diverse work force requires managers to work effectively with multiple employee perspectives.
- Because the layers of middle management are thinning out, individuals and work teams must more often "direct themselves."
- There is a growing realization that an authoritative, coercive management style does not necessarily result in productive, loyal employees. The fact that people support what they help create is behind new management approaches.

1

- People are demanding to have a strong voice in their own work lives, to have meaningful work, and to be treated with respect and dignity. They are less willing to be coerced and exploited and are speaking out against inhuman work environments.

The move toward more employee participation has resulted in the formation of many kinds of decision-making work teams. These teams are chartered, among other things, to improve quality, increase efficiencies, and strive for total customer satisfaction. Employees are being asked to do things they have not done before, and their leaders are being asked to try new ways of managing.

The increased focus on teams and employee participation requires a new leadership style and some new leadership skills. Employee participation requires leaders to be more facilitative and less controlling, to direct less and empower more. Participative leaders must know how to involve others, build consensus, and get commitment from those they lead. They must act as *facilitators,* helping others solve problems and make decisions. Employee participation calls for leaders who can use more fully than before the knowledge and experience of all employees. The participative approach requires knowledge about how to develop and lead a team and how to use group process to run an effective team meeting.

Facilitating differs from what is traditionally thought of as managing. Facilitating is not delegating or controlling others. It is not presiding at meetings or presenting information to employees. It is not solving other people's problems and making decisions for them. Instead, it is the act of *leading others to participate in what was once the domain of management.* It is the art of drawing fully on the expertise, knowledge, and experience of individuals and teams. It is the ability to capitalize on synergy to improve the way work gets done. It is knowing how to use group processes to maximize participation, productivity, and satisfaction in the workplace. Instead of managing people, a facilitative leader manages *through* people. Instead of directing and delegating, facilitators coach and enable others to act efficiently and productively.

To be sure, becoming a facilitative leader is not a step or decision but a process, and not every leader is comfortable in this role. But even autocratic managers can take some steps toward involving employees in decisions about how work gets done. In taking some first steps toward sharing the responsibility of leadership, managers and team leaders begin to let their people work *with* them as well as *for* them.

Part I

Facilitating:
A New Style of Leadership

1

The Team Movement

THE USE OF TEAMS IN ORGANIZATIONS

American companies are in transition. Managers are finding new ways to manage, organizations are being restructured, jobs are changing, and organization leaders are experimenting with new approaches to business. Emerging from this transition is a strong movement toward using teams to improve productivity, to get vital work done, and—in some cases—to be at the core of the organization.

Teams are formed for every imaginable purpose. There are quality-improvement teams, project teams, ad-hoc teams, management teams, cross-functional teams, and task forces—but all aiming to achieve something that cannot be done within the formal structure of the organization. In some cases these teams are temporary; in others they are set up to last indefinitely. In some cases they operate as an adjunct to the organization's formal hierarchy; in more experimental cases, teams are replacing the hierarchy. Companies are experimenting with giving more autonomy to "self-directed work teams" or "high-performing teams" as they are sometimes called.

Why this movement toward more reliance on teams and teamwork? Companies are finding that teams can be more responsive to the demands of a competitive marketplace than traditional hierarchies are. The rapid rate of change demands quicker response time and more flexible organizations. Continually advancing technologies make organizations and their structures obsolete before they are up and running. Intense worldwide competition drives companies to use resources more efficiently. Teams—with their flexibility and potential short-term focus—can meet this need.

As teams move into the forefront of the way American companies do business, many questions arise: What is a good team? What is the role of a team? What type of leadership is needed to maximize team productivity? Can teams really be self-directed? How do companies make the transition from traditional ways of operating to a team approach?

It is not the purpose of this book to defend the merits of teams or to support one type of organizational design over another. The best design, of course, is the one that works! Instead, this book offers suggestions and techniques for leading and facilitating teamwork in organizations. If teamwork is a better approach, as it is proving to be in many organizations, we must discover the most effective ways to develop and lead teams.

EMPLOYEE INVOLVEMENT AND PRODUCTIVITY

The team movement represents increased awareness and acknowledgment that employee involvement may be the key to improved productivity. Managers and leaders are acknowledging the fact that *people support what they help create* and that *decisions are best made at the levels where they will be carried out.*

Companies are seeking and finding ways to involve people in the vital planning and decision making that drive business. Managers are coming to realize that they cannot bear the burden of planning and decision making alone. They do not have the knowledge, time, expertise, or resources to carry out the complexities of running the business themselves. The act of sharing their responsibility with others increases the likelihood that the talent, knowledge, and experience of all employees will be used in the day-to-day operations of the business.

The success of Japanese companies throughout the world has riveted attention on the Japanese process of bottom-up, consensus decision making. American managers are more aware than ever of the need to draw fully on the vast knowledge and experience of their employees, to gain employees' help, support, and commitment up front. American managers have seen how top-down methods get bogged down in misinterpretation, poor communication, and poor decision making. As companies downsize to meet competitive demands, they expect more of individual employees.

ORGANIZATION CULTURE AND EMPLOYEE INVOLVEMENT

Increased employee involvement poses new challenges for many organizations. Cultures, especially top-down, hierarchical ones, are not accustomed to involving nonmanagerial employees in the vital work of planning, decision making, and goal setting. In these organizations, leaders tend to pass on information, delegate, and answer questions, often without seeking further involvement or creativity from subordinates. Mosvick and Nelson (1987) make this point:

> Organizations have been structured historically to reinforce authoritarian management styles.... Despite relatively recent innovations in management theory and practice (such as matrix management and quality circles), few organizations have been structured to facilitate

participation in decision making. The authoritarian organizational structure remains, for better or worse, the
most pervasive. (p. 109)[1]

Less structured organizations may be more participative
and less authoritative. In some organizations, leaders try to
involve members by asking for participation. This approach
backfires, however, when the leader does not know how to
manage their participation. In fact, some leaders ask for participation and then knowingly or unknowingly discourage it
by their actions. They may interrupt people, allow minimal
time for participation, get defensive, or simply ignore what
they hear.

In most American organizations today, communication
still mostly travels one way, with a strong focus on top-
down leadership. Employees may be encouraged to ask
questions, state opinions, and share information, but they are
seldom asked to solve problems, make decisions, create new
procedures, make plans, or find out what went wrong. To
employees, this communication pattern is frustrating—even
debilitating, if they strongly believe there are better ways to
do things. They resent being asked to support procedures
and decisions that they had no part in making.

Managers often express frustration too, complaining
that they cannot get more "participation" from subordinates
and get them to take more "real ownership" in the goals and
operations of the business. Yet these same managers often
lack the understanding and skill necessary to draw out people's ideas, listen actively, and act on employees' ideas. Un-
derneath the complaints, each of these managers really
believes in being the "leader," the one who must make all
the decisions and know everything that is going on. As these

managers and leaders become more comfortable with the fact that people support what they help create, more focus groups, work teams, ad-hoc task forces, and cross-functional teams will be formed.

THE CHANGING ROLE OF THE MANAGER

As companies flatten their hierarchies, the middle layer of management disappears or thins out. This sort of restructuring affects individuals and organizations in several ways. First, organizations must decide which middle-management activities are redundant and can be dropped and which activities must be carried out by others. Jobs must be redesigned, functions and structures must be folded together, and new duties must be added to people's existing jobs. A team may take on the responsibilities of a manager whose position has gone away. Former managers may be reclassified to the status of team member.

Thus restructuring means that former managers must adapt to new situations and acquire new skills. They may have to begin thinking and acting like team members instead of relying on their former authority. The roles of those who remain in management positions must also change. Without the middle layers of management, upper-level managers will not be able to delegate tasks or communicate with others through intermediaries. They will be closer to the ranks and, in many instances, will manage large groups of people without a middle-management buffer.

The remaining managers will therefore need team leadership and group-facilitation skills. They will benefit from seeing themselves as part of a team—or part of several teams—rather than as a position in a hierarchy. Reducing hierarchical distinctions puts more emphasis on the work people do and less on the titles that describe their place in the hierarchy.

As their own role changes, managers will also face other challenges of change. Their organizations will be dynamic, changing on many levels each day. In this environment, managers will need more than ever to tap the know-how and experience of their subordinates. Sayles (1990) writes:

> In this heavily change-oriented setting, the relationship between superiors and subordinates will continue to move away from the traditional hierarchical conception of "us" and "them." ... Not only is the work force in most industries becoming more technically well trained, but the incidence of change requires that the subordinate's know-how be tapped. The only way that these changes get implemented is when the inevitable contradictions, planning errors, and omissions are addressed by those most expert in getting things to happen: those on the firing line. (p. 9)[2]

Sayles further notes that managers may need to get more, not less, involved with the work of subordinates:

> Managers have to learn to both involve others and to get involved themselves in ways that do not injure the pride or sense of responsibility of subordinates. Until recently, a manager was often put down because he or she was too interested in nuts and bolts. We would venture a guess that in this decade, we will come full circle. The distant, hands-off executive will be the one to be criticized. (p. 9)[3]

---

[2] From "Leadership for the Nineties: Challenge and Change" by L.R. Sayles, Spring 1990, *Issues and Observations*, pp. 8-11, Greensboro, NC: Center for Creative Leadership. Reprinted by permission.

[3] Reprinted, by permission, from L.R. Sayles, "Leadership for the Nineties: Challenge and Change."

Managers in the future will also need to be more self-reliant when it comes to leading groups and teams. In the past, managers have used internal and external consultants to help with team building and team problem solving. As organizations come to depend more heavily on teams, group leadership will become an important managerial role. Relying on outside consultants for this important function will be counterproductive.

THE MANAGER AS TEAM LEADER

For teams to be successful, they must be led. "Managers" who are making the transition to "team leaders"—whether in title, concept, or both—will not only need to undergo significant changes in mind-set but will also need to make significant changes in the role they play. They will become *facilitators of teamwork.*

When one thinks of the traditional manager, one thinks of a decision maker, a delegator, a director, and often a scheduler of the work of others. When one thinks of a team leader, one thinks more of a motivator. A team leader gets individuals to work closely together on defined projects in defined time frames. When one thinks of a team and its leader, the leader is not always the most prominent figure. From time to time one or more team members take on heroic qualities by doing something dramatically good for the team. For example, in sports the players usually receive the recognition, even though the coach of a team may become a national figure. Frequently the coach is in the background.

One company the author works with is changing the title "supervisor" to "team leader." With that title change, it hopes to change the role as well, from directive to facilitative. At one training session, supervisors who were becoming team leaders, most of whom had been with the company for over ten years, listed what they thought were the characteristics of past, present, and future supervisors. Here are their lists:

Former Supervisors

- Authoritative
- "Whip and chair" disciplinarian
- Everything structured
- Employees not paid to think
- Employees expected to keep quiet
- Things catered to mood of supervisor
- Used threats
- Had "pet" people, showed favoritism
- Not good at giving feedback
- Did not know about the work, the area
- Did not counsel
- One-way, top-down, poor communicators
- Few people skills
- Knew all answers
- Little, if any, communication with other departments and functions
- Had extra privileges
- "Who you know, not what you knew"
- Sexist behaviors
- Kept tight control
- Task oriented
- Pushed quantity, not quality
- Strict on safety issues
- Generally filled their managers' expectations

Current Supervisors (1989)

- Better educated (outside and inside the company)
- More open and friendly
- Better listeners
- More conscious of quality

- Receptive to ideas of others
- More participative environment
- Two-way communication
- Better people skills
- More caring
- Encourage employees to share ideas
- Allow more independence
- More cross-communication (with other departments and functions)

Future Supervisors ("Team Leaders")

- Facilitator
- Skilled at helping groups solve problems
- Know how to develop, maintain, and motivate teams
- A model of what is expected
- Listen well
- Encourage others to participate in decisions, plans
- Can pitch in and do some of what team members do
- Understand how to coach, motivate, inspire
- Know how to get people to focus
- Work to get resources for the team (a "boundary spanner")
- Good communicator
- Skilled at developing team to high level of performance (where supervisor is no longer needed)
- Empathize with what the team struggles with
- No longer the "expert"
- Comfortable with relying on expertise of others
- Understand change
- More "computer aided"
- Can sort through information and draw conclusions

2

The New Leader-Facilitator

POWER AND THE CHANGING ROLE OF THE MANAGER

What is happening to power as the role of the manager changes and teams become more important? In the past, one of the key motivators for managers and would-be managers was power. After years of being managed and controlled by someone else in the organization, employees considered promotion to the ranks of management the pinnacle of success. They relished the power to direct and control others, often in the same style they had been directed and controlled.

The rise to power in the organizational hierarchy was reinforced by the authority and perquisites bestowed on those in higher positions. People aspired to positions of management because these positions came with more status, recognition, and money. With status, recognition, and money came success in American terms, and with that kind of success came the power to influence others, to exercise freedom and independence to a greater extent than ever before. Many erroneously believed that the road to management was the road to job security as well.

Recently many of these assumptions have been challenged. To cut back on costs and improve efficiencies, companies began to examine the cost of management. The necessity of some management positions was questioned, and some positions were eliminated as companies reorganized and as technical advances did away with people's jobs. The job security that once came with a management position has been challenged. Managers today do not necessarily have secure careers.

Another thing that has affected managerial power is the dynamic nature of business today. Change happens so quickly and information increases and fluctuates so much that managers have to rely on those they lead for information. Since information is a form of power in an organization, the manager cannot now hold all the power. Today, managerial power comes not from being the expert and knowing it all but from being able to tap the resources of others.

FROM OVERRESPONSIBILITY TO SHARED RESPONSIBILITY

For teams to be more productive, leaders must draw people out, listen, and incorporate their ideas. The idea that the leader is the only decision maker is a mind-set that has to change. The more progressive leaders are those who think of themselves as "facilitators" or "catalysts"—servants or helpers of the group.

Bradford and Cohen (1984), in their book *Managing for Excellence*, describe how an "overresponsible leader" can diminish the effectiveness of his or her subordinates (see Figure 1). In their model, the overcontrolling leader gets less and less from subordinates because the subordinates have not participated enough in all levels of decision making. As a result, they become less and less committed to the results. In turn, the overresponsible leader takes on too much ownership for what gets done. In the end, group members are not fully committed to what is planned or decided.

To overcome this tendency to be overly responsible, to take charge as if holding a horse by the reins, leaders need to

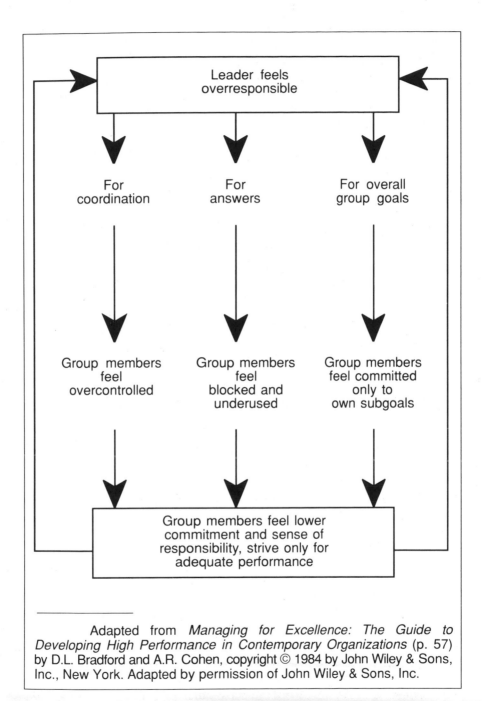

Figure 1. Consequences of the Controlling Leadership Style

place a higher value on the knowledge and experience of all group members. Gordon (1977) suggests:

> *Effective leaders must behave in such a way that they come to be perceived almost as another group member; at the same time they must help all group members feel as free as the leader to make contributions and perform needed functions in the group.* (pp. 42-43)[4]

The new leader-facilitator focuses on creating a workplace that encourages everyone to take responsibility for the success of the company. The manager becomes a partner with employees, and employees take on a partnership role with management. Managers encourage decision making at lower levels, and employees are asked to assume bigger responsibilities. There is less of a "we-they" approach to managing and more of a synergy between management and employees. To a leader-facilitator, the group is a synergistic body of diverse and valuable knowledge and experience.

CONTROLLING VERSUS FACILITATING

Understanding the role of the new leader-facilitator is easier if we look at leadership on a continuum. At one end of the continuum is the autocratic, controlling leader; at the other end is the facilitative leader. A leader's position along this continuum depends on how much he or she shares the responsibility for decision making with subordinates.

The functions and behaviors of the controlling leader differ greatly from those of the facilitative leader (see Figure 2). On the controlling side of the continuum, the leader retains full responsibility for the work and decisions of the

---

[4] From *Leader Effectiveness Training (L.E.T.): The No-Lose Way to Release the Productive Potential of People* by T. Gordon, 1977, Ridgefield, CT: Wyden. Reprinted by permission.

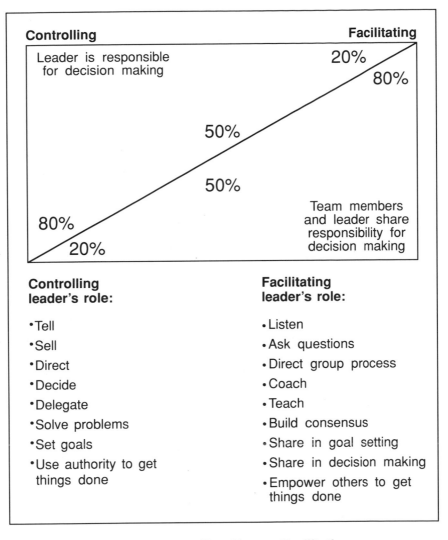

**Figure 2. Controlling Versus Facilitating
Styles of Leadership**

team. On the facilitating side of the continuum, the leader shares that responsibility with team members. The controlling leader tells, sells, directs, decides, delegates, solves problems, and rewards people. He or she tries to control the work and the output of the team. The facilitating leader listens, empowers, supports, coaches, teaches, collaborates, and strives for consensus.

A controlling, coercive style of leadership has several harmful effects. For instance, subordinates of authoritarian leaders are reluctant to reveal problems because they fear the unpleasant consequences that may result. Authoritarian approaches reduce the frequency of upward communication and affect the accuracy of communication from employees to their bosses. In fact, group members selectively send the messages that they think will bring rewards and forestall punishment. "Tell the boss what he or she wants to hear" is the principle governing their behavior. According to Gordon (1977, p. 160), "Power most seriously produces counterproductive behavior when coercive behavior of the leader tangibly reduces the effectiveness of a group member...."[5] Gordon presents these other, equally harmful outcomes of an authoritarian approach:

- Group members try to get on the good side of their leader or become "leader's pets."
- Excessive competitiveness and rivalry among group members results in tattling, backbiting, cheating, covering up, and gossiping. These power struggles arise out of the need for individuals to avoid punishment and to look good in the leader's eyes.
- Group members cope with power through submission and conformity and become weak in initiative and creativity, a development that is counterproductive to problem solving and risk taking.
- Those who fail to submit and conform may become rebellious and defiant, thereby frustrating other group members and weakening the work of the group.

---

[5] From *Leader Effectiveness Training (L.E.T.): The No-Lose Way to Release the Productive Potential of People* by T. Gordon, 1977, Ridgefield, CT: Wyden. Reprinted by permission.

- Others may choose to withdraw from the group relationship, either physically or psychologically. They may refuse to speak up or get involved for fear of punishing consequences.

The leader who operates on the controlling end of the continuum takes power into his or her hands and produces results, many of which are based on his or her own abilities. The facilitating leader puts the power into everyone's hands, serving as a guide and a catalyst. The facilitating leader also produces results. The difference: The facilitating leader's power is shared and often expanded because of the synergy of people's working together. Thus the facilitating leader, together with others, often produces better results. Instead of giving up power, the facilitating leader expands and shares power.

The controlling leader is more likely to see power as limited. The facilitating leader is more likely to view power as dynamic and expansive, maybe even infinite. To the facilitating leader, power is not something to be fought over but something to use to achieve a greater goal.

Under facilitative leaders, group members are more motivated to support the decisions that are made, because they feel the decisions are theirs and not someone else's. Responsibility for carrying out the decision is shared too. Group members' talents, experience, and knowledge are therefore better employed. Managers and leaders have more relevant information. Management and the group develop more trust and more overall group cohesiveness.

In facilitated teams, everyone has a chance to be and feel powerful. The goal is not to gain power but to complete the work assigned to the team. The goal is not to divide power into definable pieces but to work together to produce what could not be produced by individuals working alone.

It is the leader's view of power that governs his or her leadership style. A controlling leader views power as limited, as something to be possessed by an elite few. The facilitating leader views power as expansive, a positive force to be shared for the increased good of the organization.

MYTHS ABOUT FACILITATION

Like anything that is not fully understood, the concept of facilitation conjures up, for some people, images of support groups, "touchy-feely" team-building sessions, and the venting of frustrations. Some of the common myths about facilitation follow, along with the realities of how it works.

"Facilitation is a loose approach to management that invites disorder and chaos." On the contrary, a well-facilitated team has clear boundaries and ground rules. Within those boundaries, however, there is room for creativity and flexibility. Facilitating leaders spend time planning how they will work with their people, how meetings will be run, and how issues will be communicated and dealt with. When they invite participation, they do so within a structure that will ensure productivity. In fact, good facilitators place a high value on both structure and creativity.

"A facilitative leader simply agrees to everything the team wants; truly strong and powerful leaders would not want to appear weak in front of their people and would therefore not ask for help and support." On the contrary, to be a facilitative leader takes strength of character and a strong sense of oneself. It takes courage and wisdom to allow others to make decisions and to support those decisions. It takes a strong person to set clear boundaries without destroying team morale. It takes wisdom to determine correctly which decisions can better be made by the team and which must be reserved for management. It takes a strong person to seek advice and input from others and still make the best decision.

"Facilitative leaders give up their power and control." Actually, they have access to more power, because they empower others to act; they get power from the people they lead. Facil-

itative leadership increases the power of a team as a whole and the sphere of influence for that team. Facilitators do not give up control; rather, they control things (like meetings) in such a way that others will produce their highest quality work.

"It won't work in this culture!" Many corporate cultures are not very receptive to participation and involvement on the part of their people. Yet determined leaders can gradually and quietly introduce participation and involvement. In one-on-one meetings, the leader-facilitator can demonstrate a willingness to listen and to explore the merits of an idea before judging it. Decisions reached in group meetings can be designated "team decisions."

"Facilitation takes too much time. We won't get anything done." Some people fear that the team approach requires too many meetings in which too much time is spent hearing everyone out and arguing every point. Facilitation does encourage individual expression, discussion, and even disagreement. Within a planned meeting structure, however, participation can be—and should be—highly productive. Building consensus takes more time initially, but in the long run, consensus means more support and commitment from those who must make something happen.

"Facilitation encourages anarchy." Again, with guidance and structure provided by the facilitator, people can focus on the issue and deal within the realm of their authority. On the other hand, for facilitation to work, some decisions still need to filter down from management to workers. This is not anarchy; this is involved decision making.

"The democracy of facilitation will water down the quality of decisions." This has not been true in Japan. The bottom-up, decision-by-consensus process ensures that decisions made by Japanese businesses are well thought out, realistic, and motivating to employees. Once team members decide to act, support has already been rallied. Japanese businesses do not experience that great time lag between the making of a

decision at the top and its implementation at the bottom, as is common in American businesses. The time is put in up front, in gathering support and building consensus.

"Once we start a facilitative approach, we will have to do everything this way." On the contrary, some decisions can be reserved for certain levels or roles. In fact, facilitative leaders can take a strong stand about the situations that call for participation and those that do not. However, most companies have erred in the other direction: not allowing enough decisions to be made by employees. When a facilitative approach works well, people can be expected to want to use it frequently. Leaders will have to determine when facilitation is appropriate.

WHAT IS A LEADER-FACILITATOR?

A leader-facilitator is someone who bears in mind the philosophy that *a leader does not do for others what they can do for themselves.* A leader-facilitator is someone who:

- Listens actively;
- Asks questions and listens to the whole answer;
- Reserves judgment and keeps an open mind;
- Actively seeks other ideas and opinions;
- Encourages different viewpoints;
- Teaches others how to solve problems, without solving the problems for them;
- Teaches and coaches others, without telling them what to do;
- Organizes information and data so others can understand and act on it;
- Models the behavior he or she would like to see in others;
- Knows how to bring the right people together for a task;
- Is aware of his or her own limitations and knows who is better qualified to make a decision or complete a task;

- Helps people reach consensus and strives for win-win agreements;
- Does not take personal credit for what other individuals or the team does but ensures that credit goes where credit is due;
- Understands that diversity can affect teamwork in positive ways;
- Understands that different people are motivated by different things and is willing to work hard to address these individual needs;
- Shares power and authority with others;
- Encourages team members to take responsibility for issues, problems, actions, and projects;
- Looks for ways to help the team achieve its goals;
- Finds opportunities to reward appropriate behavior; minimizes punishment for inappropriate behavior;
- Is firm about goals and flexible about the process used to reach those goals;
- Has belonged to and had positive work experience with heterogeneous groups (has not been solely with people who are like himself or herself);
- Is not afraid to address conflict; and
- Understands and acknowledges that people's individual needs (social, personal, career, lifestyle, work preferences, and so on) affect teamwork and works with, not against, these needs.

BALANCING MANAGING WITH FACILITATING

Using a facilitating style does not mean that managers and team leaders stop doing all those things they used to do. Managers must still prepare budgets, project work volume, analyze costs, solve problems, hire people, and give performance reviews. The facilitating leader, however, does not do it all alone. Facilitative team leaders build teams that can share the leadership and management responsibilities. Management duties still exist; the way they are carried out is what changes.

For example, in a facilitative organization some decisions will still be left to one person, perhaps the manager or team leader. The facilitative manager or team leader, however, consults with others before making such decisions. The information available for making decisions is richer, and therefore the decisions are better.

Daniels (1986) describes two types of group decision making, consultative and consensus:

> A consultative decision making process is one in which the members of the group have been asked to provide their information and interpretations, but *one member*— perhaps the leader—reserves the right to make the final decision. By using the group's resources, the deciding member enriches his or her own decision-making process.... A consensus decision-making process...is achieved when *all members* of the group agree that it is the best possible decision given their information base and its evaluation. Every member has the authority to veto the decision until, in fact, each member has found it possible to agree on a rational basis. (p. 10)

By deciding which decisions are to be made through consultation and which by consensus, the manager or team leader exercises his or her managerial responsibility. Indeed, a difficult part of managing in a facilitative style is determining what type of decision process a situation calls for. The manager still remains accountable for the final decision, even though he or she may not have made the decision.

Empowering others to take part in decisions does not mean that employees will automatically make quality decisions. People must want to take part; in other words, they need to be *motivated* to do so. They need to feel there is something in it for them.

Even though they may be motivated to participate, employees may not always have the *ability* to make a decision.

Managers and team leaders need to help employees gain the knowledge and skills necessary to participate in decision making.

And even when the ability and motivation are present, employees may still not be able to participate unless they are given the *permission*, support, and resources to do so—in other words, the authority to participate in a productive way. For example, teams may be formed and given the training and motivation to increase the number of decisions they make. However, their decision-making power is in reality nonexistent if they are limited in the amount of time they can meet or are told they cannot have any money to make changes or are not given audience with supervisors. If they are given a job to do without the authority to do it, motivation dies and knowledge and skills are not put to use for the good of the organization.

Facilitative managers and team leaders do not give up their role; on the contrary, they have important responsibilities. They have to see that things are in place for participation to be productive. They have to make sure that participation is worthwhile and will make a difference to employees (the motivation), that people's knowledge and skills are assessed and upgraded (the ability), and that people have sufficient resources and authority to participate (the permission).

Part II

How Facilitation Works

3

Getting People to Work Together

OLD AND NEW PARADIGMS

The manager's role historically grew out of the need for someone to supervise and coordinate the work of others. The manager's job was to hire, motivate, and direct the work of several individuals so certain tasks would get done. In some cases teamwork was called for, but in many cases, individuals were given a job to do without the need to interact regularly with others. As jobs grew more complex, more specialists were needed. When a new job needed to be done, a new position was created and someone hired to fill that position.

What we see in many organizations today is the result of that growth of individual positions. In many organizations a lot of individuals do a lot of different tasks. In general, people work apart—each on his or her own tasks—coming together only to inform one another or to solve a problem pertaining to the whole group. The work of the group as a whole is overseen and directed by the manager.

Several "old paradigms" have justified managing people this way:

- The manager is the technical expert.
- The manager makes final decisions.
- The manager uses an autocratic style.

- The manager imposes controls on employees.
- The manager defines how work will get done.
- The manager processes all information and communicates it to employees.
- The manager sets and interprets the group's goals.
- The manager administers rewards and punishments.
- People are expendable.
- Employees need only a few skills to do their jobs.
- The focus is on specialization.
- The organization is concerned only with its own purpose.
- Manager-employee relationships are based on a "we" and "they" distinction.
- People operate within narrow job definitions.
- The organization is structured hierarchically.
- Teams are formed when needed.
- Technology drives the organization's activities.
- The work force is homogeneous.
- Change is the exception, not the rule.

Much has happened to dramatize the limitations of these old paradigms. Managers have not been able to keep up with technical advances and new information. Therefore, their former role as experts has become outdated, and they must now rely heavily on technical experts for help in making technical decisions. In fact, managers can no longer even be expected to set the group's goals single-handedly.

The old paradigms defined individuals' roles narrowly. The strong focus on specialization and the narrow definition of people's jobs made it almost impossible to solve problems that involve several jobs, functions, departments, or—in many cases—divisions or even companies. Too many problems fell between the cracks—between jobs or functions—and no one was there to solve them. An overfocus on specialization led to the attitude expressed in "That's not my job," a problem that has caused vast inefficiencies in business today.

When managers and their people set up "we-they" boundaries, the result was more adversarial than cooperative. The old paradigms created tension, which often caused management and employees to counter each other.

The old paradigms also placed a great deal of emphasis on doing the task without addressing the important social dimension of teamwork and organizational work life. Older methods therefore often failed to get enough commitment from employees to get jobs done.

When people's jobs are defined narrowly, they can get by with having fewer skills and being trained to do only a few things well. Such limitations create a less flexible work force, although the times require more flexibility. Also, narrow job definition causes employees to work in isolation from one another. Frequently, people know very little about what others do, about what the company as a whole does, and about how their jobs affect those of others. As a result, it is difficult to get people to solve complex problems involving several jobs or departments. Worst of all, the old methods fail to take full advantage of employees' abilities.

Organizations today are faced with unprecedented change on every front. The inability to adapt easily and quickly causes problems in all aspects of organizational life. The old paradigms, with their less flexible structures and employees, have made organizational change slow and painful.

Because the old paradigms do not deal effectively with change, some new paradigms are working their way into organizations. Companies are experimenting with these new attitudes to varying degrees and with varying degrees of success. Nonetheless, these new paradigms are evolving:

- Employees are experts possessing unique technical knowledge and skills.

- Employees are the natural ones to make some decisions.

- Controls are minimized or set collectively.

- Employees participate in defining how work gets done.
- Employees participate in setting and interpreting group goals.
- People are resources to be developed and used fully.
- Jobs are defined broadly and entail multiple skills.
- Employees focus on applying special knowledge to larger problems.
- The organization is concerned with members' and society's purposes as well as its own.
- "Partnership" relationships are fostered between managers and employees.
- Teamwork is structured into the organization.
- Teams are used to take advantage of synergy.
- Teams take over some of the work of managers.
- Organization structures are flatter.
- People are given larger boundaries and encouraged to develop more skills.
- The organization is customer driven.
- The work force is diverse.
- Change is the norm.

The new paradigms mean a more flexible and knowledgeable work force, with problem solving and decision making shared by all.

A NEW ROLE FOR EMPLOYEES

Under the old paradigms, employees had few decisions to make and relied heavily on the manager to direct their work. Under the new paradigms, employees take on more responsibility, moving into areas once reserved for management. Just as management's role changes in participative companies, so does the role of employees.

Even though people say they want to participate more in company decisions, when given this opportunity they may hold back. There are several reasons for this. First, they simply may lack the skills and the experience to assess alternatives, gather data, make decisions, plan changes, and solve more complex problems. Second, they may fear the consequences if they make mistakes. Third, they may not trust management's new approach and may hold back to see if people really will be rewarded (and not punished) for participation. Fourth, they may not be used to working in teams and may have difficulty sharing their work with others or establishing good team relationships.

Therefore, when management decides to involve its people in more decision making, it is really asking individuals to play a different role than before. This difficult change needs to be approached step by step. People need to be given not only the *authority* to make decisions but also the *means* (the skills, training, and support). In addition, they must have a desire to play a more participative role. Without adequate *motivation*, people will not change the way they have been operating. Management needs to provide the incentives.

THE VALUE OF TEAMWORK

Effective teamwork can address two key problems with the old paradigms. First, under the old paradigms, the talents of individual employees were often not fully used, and the organization suffered as a result. Second, the isolation of individuals meant that organizations failed to capitalize on synergy, the effect of working to achieve something collectively that could not have been achieved through individual efforts. The output of group work is, in many instances, greater than the combined output of its individual members working alone.

Organizations are beginning to realize that allowing people to work alone does not yield the return on investment that the organization needs to succeed in today's competitive marketplace. Because of the complexity of today's business problems and the continual change faced by organizations, the resources of all employees must be available when appropriate and necessary. Leaders must be able to rely on the wisdom of the group to solve not just the occasional mind-boggling problem but also the ongoing, day-to-day concerns faced by every organization.

TEN ESSENTIALS OF TEAMWORK

What makes a collection of people become a team? What keeps team members working well together? What do groups need to function productively? A team can be defined as a collection of individuals formed to carry out a set of tasks or to accomplish a goal. Team members have mutually interdependent purposes, so that the success of one team member is contingent on the success of others. In addition, each person has a sense of belonging or membership, and all team members accept certain behaviors based on group norms, procedures, and constraints.

Studies in group dynamics (what goes on among people in group settings) show that teams or groups have certain key needs (see Figure 3). For a team to stay alive and function well, these needs must be met:

Common goals. Members of a team need a reason for being and working together. The goals of a team rationalize its existence. Although the goals may change over time, each member should clearly understand what these goals are at any point. The less clear the goals are, the more likely it is that they will be misinterpreted by team members and the more likely it is that the group will suffer internal tensions, arguments, and cross-purposes. Without clear goals, people become apathetic or use the group to achieve their own personal goals.

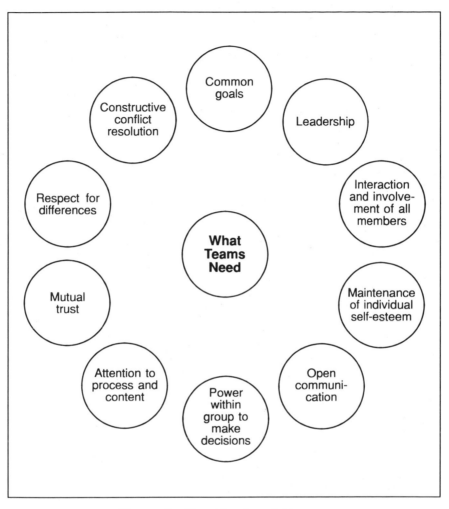

Figure 3. Key Needs of Teams

Leadership. Teams need leaders and members who can lead when necessary. Whether a group has a formal leader or leadership is shared, the group needs people who are willing to take the risk of leadership. Leaders are the people who are respected and influential enough to get others to listen to them, to get support from reluctant members, and to build bridges with groups and people outside the team. Leaders help coordinate the work of the team, have good communication skills, and know how to get everyone involved.

Interaction and involvement of all members. To achieve synergy and group spirit, all team members must contribute actively. Holding back creates problems for the team. Therefore, it is important for team leaders to know how to get everyone involved.

Maintenance of individual self-esteem. The good of the group should not prevail to the point that members lose self-esteem. Each person's contribution must be heard, valued, and acknowledged. Favoritism must be avoided, and members must be encouraged to be themselves. The challenge to the team and to the leader is to enhance, not lower, the self-esteem of each member.

Open communication. Team members need to feel they can speak their minds, that the channels of communication are open to everyone—especially to the leader. The team should have ample time to communicate; share information; discuss issues; and use informal communication channels to pass on information, make suggestions, and bring up new ideas.

Power within the group to make decisions. The work of the team should center around the things it has the power to influence. Giving teams work to do that does not get approved for implementation is unproductive and demotivating. Some of the failure of early quality circles in this country can be traced to the fact that the suggestions they made were sometimes either ignored or vetoed higher up. These teams were not given the power to carry out the work they were asked to do. If more decisions were made at the level where they were carried out, people would have more reasons to work together in teams.

Attention to both process and content. For people to function well together as a group, attention must be paid both to the process used to do the work and to the content of the work or the group's task. Process includes attention to how people get along together, how the work is structured and distributed, and what the general rules of working together are. Usually, the task to be done gets a lot of attention, while the process of how the team members work together is expected to fall into place. Because process problems may hurt feelings and impede progress, it is best to address the team's process along with its tasks.

Mutual trust. Trust depends on how the leader and members treat one another. When something happens to break that trust (a commitment not met, a confidentiality betrayed, dishonesty), it can be difficult to retrieve. Members and the team leader may need to discuss how their behaviors and attitudes affect trust. Then everyone will need to try to do those things that will build and maintain trust.

Respect for differences. Team members need to feel they can disagree and be different from others without being punished. The leader sets the tone, but each member has to take responsibility for acknowledging and respecting the needs of others. When individuals on a team are not getting some of their needs met, teamwork becomes demotivating for them.

Constructive conflict resolution. Conflict is natural. When it surfaces, it must be addressed in a healthy way. Again, the leader plays an important role in getting group members to express conflict and come to general agreement. Unresolved conflict leads to less-than-adequate performance, resentments, and lack of motivation.

TASK AND SOCIAL DIMENSIONS OF TEAMWORK

Teamwork has two dimensions: task and social. These two dimensions are inseparable, for without either, teamwork does not exist. The task dimension refers to the work that team members are to perform—the jobs they have to do and how they are going to do those jobs. The social dimension refers to how team members feel toward one another and their membership on the team. At any given point in the team's work, both the task and social dimensions operate. When team members make a decision and develop ideas, they are simultaneously developing ways to get along together.

Team leaders benefit by addressing regularly both the social and task needs of their teams. To the extent the team does its tasks well, it will be productive. To the extent it manages its relationships well, team members will have a sense of belonging and commitment.

PRESERVING THE DIGNITY OF THE INDIVIDUAL

Leaders will do well to think of a team as a collection of diverse individuals, each with his or her own unique character and potential for contribution to the group. Being expected to conform and to subjugate individual needs and desires for the common good is degrading to team members. The fact is that some people are more comfortable as part of a group than others. Some more independent members may feel constrained and ill at ease working in a team. Others, because of their race, sex, age, religion, or culture, may not have much in common with other members and yet feel pressured to get along and conform. An effective leader is sensitive to the need to preserve individual dignity, to capitalize on differences, and to not try to achieve conformity.

A facilitative leader views teamwork as an ongoing negotiation among diverse individuals who are all working toward common goals. The skills of facilitation help leaders blend different views into consensus so the team can achieve its goals. The effective team leader acknowledges individual differences and challenges the team to meet as many individual needs as possible while achieving the team's goals.

4

Making the Transition
from Controlling to Facilitating

BASIC PRINCIPLES FOR INITIATING CHANGE

Moving from a controlling to a facilitative style means
change: changes in mind-set and leadership style, changes in
the way leaders relate to their followers and followers relate
to leaders, changes in the way work gets done, changes in
the types of behavior and performance that are rewarded,
and changes in the way team members relate to one another.
There is no easy way to tackle all of these changes at once,
nor will the transition be a smooth one.

Leaders who are making the transition to a more facilitative approach will do well to remember three principles of
change:

- Change takes *time.*
- Change is a *process*, not a decision.
- Change requires plenty of *experience and practice* in the
  new way of doing things.

Leaders seeking change must acknowledge the vast effort it
takes and must not give up when it takes more time and
practice than anticipated. Change is not on a switch, like a
light that goes on and off, but is a process—sometimes a very
long one. Leaders who effectively implement change make
sure that their teams have plenty of opportunities to practice

new ways of doing things while they go about their day-to-day activities.

Here are some additional principles that will help leaders make the transition to facilitation:

- Make one or two changes at a time. Do not tackle everything at once.
- Allow time for change to take place. Change is never easy, and people need time to learn new ways of working together.
- Reward people's efforts to change; otherwise, they will not change.
- Keep the goal in mind. The goal is not to have a team but to increase productivity and employee satisfaction.
- Accomplish something daily toward the goal. Do not let time go by without moving in the desired direction.
- Use planning and regular evaluation of progress as tools to move toward the goal.
- Have patience with people. Change is difficult and even threatening for some.
- Do not play God. Be realistic but positive about what you can accomplish given your company's culture and the constraints placed on you. Acknowledge that you cannot change the organization alone, and plan accordingly.

Perhaps you want to make some changes in your leadership style but still have a nagging question: "Where do I start?" You may feel overwhelmed by the number of things you want to change or not understand how to apply the ideas presented here to your own situation.

Here is a suggested process for making the transition from a controlling style of leadership to a more facilitative one. First, while reading this book, list the things you would like to change in the way your team or group works together or in how you lead the group. Think in terms of making these improvements over many months to several years. Second, ask yourself what strengths, support systems, and other resources you already have that can help you make these improvements. Plan to use these strengths to your advantage when you begin to make changes. Third, break these big changes down into small steps. If you want to start listening more to people, for example, write down the actions you can take to accomplish this goal. For example:

- Ask at least three questions of subordinates this week. Then make an effort to listen without interrupting.
- Take a course in listening.
- Ask a friend or significant other to tell you when you interrupt and when you appear to demonstrate good listening skills.

WHAT TO EXPECT

People resist change, even when it is for the better. Change disrupts people's lives, challenges their beliefs about themselves and their world, and creates confusion and disorientation. Therefore, do not expect others to welcome the "new you" or to be supportive, even when you believe you are acting this way for their benefit. In fact, you may find subordinates and followers almost antagonistic at first, even when you begin to listen more and ask for their input.

Why does this happen? When you begin to draw people out and listen to them, they may distrust you at first. They will be wary, watching for your reactions. They may simply avoid saying anything, afraid that what they say may be used against them. Unless you have been a good listener in the past, they may not be used to expressing their feelings and ideas to you.

Another typical reaction is that people will, when finally asked how they feel and think, vent many of their frustrations all at once. They will take the opportunity to talk about everything they do not like. This deluge of negativity may be difficult to deal with. But the way to handle it is to listen and take notes. Ask people for clarification or examples when they are vague, so you can more fully understand the extent of their complaints. Demonstrate your ability to listen without sermonizing and without judgment or bias. Try not to become defensive. Avoid making promises. You may explain that you are listening so you can begin to see ways to involve them more in planning and decision making, that you will be trying to help them solve some of these problems in the future.

HOW TO L.E.A.D.

Leaders can use a simple four-step model to ensure employee participation and increase productivity:

Lead with a clear purpose.

Empower to participate.

Aim for consensus.

Direct the process.

This L.E.A.D. model includes key leadership functions: setting clear goals and objectives, getting people involved, reaching consensus on important items, and paying attention to both tasks (the work) and relationships (the team).

Using this model ensures that the ten essentials of teamwork are met. Paying attention to all four parts of the model provides the *leadership* that any team needs. Leading with a clear purpose meets the need for *common goals*. Empowering members to participate achieves the high level of *interaction and involvement* that group members need. Participation and consensus help maintain *individual self-esteem* and encourage *open communication*. Participation and consensus also help build *mutual trust* and achieve a healthy *respect for differences among team members*, while providing an avenue for *construc-*

tive conflict resolution. Using all four parts of the model will assure that there is *power within the group to make decisions.* Leading with a clear purpose and directing the process ensure that leaders pay *attention to both process and content.*

The following paragraphs offer a more detailed analysis of this L.E.A.D. model.

Lead with a Clear Purpose

To lead with a clear purpose simply means to use goals as a motivator for teams. For goals to motivate people, they need to be challenging, positive, and realistic. A leader can give power and focus to the team's goals in several ways.

First, set realistic, team-oriented goals that tie to the company's goals. Team-oriented goals are ones that apply specifically to your team. They are the things your team needs to accomplish to support the larger company goals. The company's goals are not immediate enough to motivate your team. You need to help your team identify specific goals that it alone can accomplish. Make sure they support the company goals.

Next, publish those goals. Make them visible for all to see. Do not expect people to remember them if they are not discussed and referred to often. Do not bury them in occasional memos and documents. Instead, post them in meeting rooms on flip charts or posters; use stickers or other visual reminders to keep the goals in front of everyone. Refer to the goals often in memos, presentations, and meetings. Whenever possible, use the goals to guide a decision. Ask others to do the same. When someone comes to you with a problem or suggestion, say, "In light of our goal of 95 percent on-time deliveries, what do you think is the best solution?"

Work with your team to identify milestones that will show you are making progress toward your goals. Keep these subgoals in front of your people, with deadlines whenever possible. For example, you might have these milestones for the goal of achieving 95 percent on-time delivery:

- 85 percent by the end of the third quarter;
- 90 percent by the end of the fourth quarter;
- 93 percent by the end of the first quarter of next year; and
- 95 percent by the end of the second quarter of next year.

Track and report the team's progress in achieving its established goals. When a milestone is achieved, acknowledge it and celebrate it. Take a little time out to feel good about meeting a goal. Over time, allow your team to set its own goals, monitor its own progress, and plan its own celebrations.

Empower to Participate

Once goals have been established and published, your next step is to empower people to participate in achieving those goals. The word "empower" means to give power or authority, to authorize, to enable or permit. Thus it means you can begin to facilitate, to get others to determine how goals will be achieved. Even though the goals themselves may motivate the team, team members become unmotivated if they cannot participate in important decisions regarding ways to achieve those goals—especially if they are expected to carry out those decisions.

Not everyone needs to participate in every decision, but people should participate in those decisions they will have to implement. "Who will we depend on to carry out this decision?" is the key question here. Those people should at least be consulted about the decision that is made. Some decisions may naturally fall to one or two team members. Others will need to be made by the entire team. Still others may require the representation of others outside the team.

As a leader, you have at least two choices when it comes to involving your team in making a decision. One is simply to consult with team members and then make the decision yourself. Alternatively, you can work with others (one, a few, or the whole group) to come to a consensus about the decision. When a consensus decision is made, you have the option of remaining neutral and simply facilitating the decision process or becoming a member of the group making the decision. The role you choose depends on several factors, such as your comfort with letting the group decide, your ability to avoid overinfluencing the group's decision, how much you have to be involved in implementation, and whether team members want your involvement.

You have many other ways to empower people to participate. You can, of course, involve the team in setting its own goals. You may decide to redesign jobs and procedures so team members will have to interact to get work done. You can identify which types of decisions you will make and which types of decisions the team or team members will make.

One of the main principles of facilitation is to get others to solve problems they are capable of solving. You can encourage more involvement by learning techniques to get others to solve their own problems. These techniques are covered in later chapters: Chapter 5 deals with getting someone to solve his or her own problem; Chapters 6 through 12 deal with getting groups to solve problems.

Facilitative leaders encourage participation by listening more than talking and by asking more than telling. Two skills are therefore critical for good facilitators: listening and asking questions. Listening, or *active listening*, is required to hear, really hear, what the other person is saying. Active listening requires that you observe the other person as well as hear his or her words. The other person's body language, tone of voice, eye contact, and other signals will give you additional information about how that person perceives the issue. Active listening requires that your own body language indicate your receptiveness to the other person; maintaining an open posture, nodding your head, being still, keeping eye contact—all these and more show that you are paying attention. Active listening also means not being distracted by others, by the surrounding environment, or by difficulties the speaker may have in getting his or her message across. It means not thinking about what you are going to say while the other person is talking. It also means that instead of jumping ahead to judge the other person or figure out why his or her remarks are not valid, you must postpone judgment until you have heard that person out. (Chapter 5 presents more on active listening.)

Unfortunately, sometimes we are a bit lazy or too preoccupied to listen. We may be pressured with other issues. We may be feeling down or defensive or have a hard time being patient while the other person talks. We may wish we were somewhere else. Or we may misunderstand the other person. Here is where another aspect of active listening comes into play. In addition to knowing how to listen, we need to know when to ask questions or clarify what the other person has been saying. We can repeat a brief version of what we thought was said, or *paraphrase*, to check out the accuracy of our interpretation. Or we may ask the person to give us more information or help clear up our confusion. Generally it is best to give the other person a chance to talk, to formulate his or her thoughts, and to finish what he or she wants to say before jumping in with questions. Such patience is a rare commodity in a busy, pressured, rapidly changing world; but it is nonetheless a highly important trait for good listeners—and especially for good leaders.

Another way to empower team members is to regularly seek their ideas, opinions, and reactions without judging or punishing them for what they say. This is in fact a very simple habit to get into, but it is often overlooked. Leaders are often busy people, and some do not get a lot of opportunity to interact with their people. A good leader-facilitator, however, will make time to seek others' opinions and ideas, even if only for a few minutes in the hall. Stopping by a person's office for the sole purpose of getting his or her opinion is particularly empowering for that person. You might say something like "Jan, I'm interested in your opinion of the Blair account. What do you think we should do to improve that situation?"

Once you have asked someone else's opinion, the next few steps are critical. You must:

1. Listen actively.
2. Ask questions or paraphrase to clarify what was said.
3. Thank the person, and *resist having the last word.*

Sometimes you will be tempted to offer your opinion (especially if the other person asks for it). But remember that one of the best ways you can empower others to speak up is to listen without having the final word. Staying neutral for a while frees others to express their true opinions. Because you are the leader, your opinion can sway others. If you really want to hear what others think, let them talk without trying to influence them or being defensive.

Another empowering technique is to avoid letting others rely on you for answers. Instead, when someone comes to you for an answer or decision, ask what he or she thinks. Using this technique does not mean you do not have an opinion or are abdicating your leadership role. It means you are encouraging others to solve their own problems. You are giving them permission—empowering them—to take on some of the leadership role.

Leaders who empower their teams to make decisions must then support those decisions. If you must help implement the decision, then you should be involved in the decision-making process along with everyone else. But even if you do not need to be involved, you still need to support your team once the decision is made. Support comes in many forms: having a positive attitude, offering your assistance, running interference, explaining to your superiors what your team is doing, and giving encouragement.

Another way to encourage participation is to give the team regular opportunities (probably at team meetings) to assess itself. You are not the only one to measure the team's performance. Teach the team members how to measure their own performance. When assessing itself, the team should cover both how well it is achieving its goals and how well it is doing as a team. Are good relationships being built among team members? Is there a spirit of cooperation? Are members working out differences in acceptable ways? What team norms (ground rules) are working? What norms need to be changed or added?

Finally, become proficient at giving genuinely positive reinforcement to your team members. Watch for things they are doing well, and let them know that you appreciate what they have done. Here are some general principles to follow when giving praise:

- Be specific about what you are praising.

- Be timely; do not wait too long after the event or behavior.

- Keep the praise separate from problems or negative concerns; it may get lost if it is sandwiched between problems.

- Give praise regularly but not so often that it becomes expected or meaningless.

Aim for Consensus

The third step in the L.E.A.D. model, aim for consensus, means helping people move toward general agreement. Foster consensus throughout the process of working with others, not just as a final step. Expect conflicts, but treat them as natural and work through them. Your role in building consensus is to bring as many ideas, opinions, and conflicts to the surface as possible and then to get people to find the approach that best meets the needs of the organization and individual team members.

After getting general agreement, it is your responsibility to act on the decision or to empower the group to act on it. You may use the group's input to make a decision yourself, or you may let the group's decision stand.

Direct the Process

The last step in the L.E.A.D. model, direct the process, requires experience in working with groups and knowledge about the group process. An effective leader will use various techniques, many discussed in the following chapters, to help the group get its work done.

CONCLUSION

Figure 4 (see page 54) lists the important group needs met during each step of the L.E.A.D. model and lists key tasks that must be performed by the leader and by team members. The L.E.A.D. model provides ample opportunity for employees to take part in the management of their organizations and gives leaders a critical role to play in making this happen.

Leader Functions	Group Needs Met	Leader Tasks	Team-Member Tasks
Lead with a clear purpose	• Common goals • Attention to content • Leadership	• Set boundaries • Interpret company goals • Facilitate team's setting of its own goals • Evaluate and track progress toward goals	• Ask questions to test own understanding • Participate in setting goals for team • Help leader track and evaluate progress toward goals
Empower to participate	• High level of involvement of all members • Maintenance of self-esteem • Leadership • Respect for differences • Trust	• Ask questions • Listen • Show understanding • Summarize • Seek divergent viewpoints • Record ideas	• Contribute ideas from own experience and knowledge • Listen to others • Build on others' ideas • Consider others' ideas • Ask questions • Think creatively
Aim for consensus	• Constructive conflict resolution • Power within group to make decisions • Leadership • Trust	• Use group-process techniques (brainstorming, problem solving, prioritization, etc.) • Ask questions • Listen • Seek common interests • Summarize • Confront in constructive way	• Focus on common interests and goals • Listen to and consider others' ideas • Make own needs known • Disagree in constructive way
Direct the process	• Attention to process • Leadership • Trust	• Give clear directions • Intervene to keep group on track • Read group and adjust • Remain neutral • Suggest alternate processes to help group achieve goal	• Listen • Keep purpose in mind • Stay focused on objective • Use own energy and enthusiasm to help process along

Figure 4. Using the L.E.A.D. Model

5

Facilitating One-on-One Meetings

PURPOSES OF ONE-ON-ONE MEETINGS

Meetings between the leader and one other group member serve several key purposes. They keep the leader in touch with what is going on with each person on the team. They provide the leader an opportunity to give positive feedback, to confront problems early on, and to work collaboratively with individuals. One of the most important purposes is to give the leader a chance to show interest and concern for each person. Important work also gets done in one-on-one meetings, such as setting goals, solving problems, making decisions, bringing problems or concerns to the surface, providing support, giving feedback on progress, and building consensus.

One-on-one meetings are for issues that concern the leader and one other individual. Whenever possible, these issues should be addressed as they arise. Then, when the team members are together, they will not have unsolved individual problems to deal with.

This chapter deals with three facilitator techniques that are particularly useful in one-on-one meetings:

- Consensus building;

- Problem solving; and

- Constructive confrontation.

For clarity, these techniques are presented separately. In real life they are often used in conjunction. A good facilitator can use any one or a combination of these techniques when the situation calls for it.

BUILDING CONSENSUS ONE ON ONE

An effective leader needs to know how to reach consensus, or come to a mutually acceptable agreement, with another person. (Building consensus in a group meeting is covered in Chapter 12.) Whether the task is setting a goal, making a joint decision, or planning how to proceed on a project, building consensus is important in one-on-one settings. Here are four simple steps managers and leaders can use to facilitate the process of getting to an agreement with another person:

1. Draw out the other person's ideas.
2. Show understanding.
3. Offer your ideas.
4. Work toward a solution that will meet both people's needs.

These four steps aim for win-win, instead of win-lose, outcomes.

To achieve the first step, drawing out the other person's ideas, you should ask open-ended questions. These are questions that cannot be answered with a yes or no or a one- or two-word answer. Open-ended questions invite the other person to share opinions, ideas, and experiences that shed light on the subject. (Chapter 9 covers open-ended questions in more detail.)

After asking an open-ended question, pause for a response. While the other person is speaking, listen *actively*. Listening actively is a complex skill that many people do not fully understand. To listen actively you must be alert and nonjudgmental. Here are some things you must do:

- Listen to every word.
- Watch for nonverbal clues that will help you get the full meaning of what the other person is saying.
- Avoid distractions: your own fidgeting, noise, phone calls, and so on.
- Use eye contact, head nodding, and an attentive posture to show that you are listening.
- Avoid thinking ahead to what you are going to say.
- Do not interrupt.
- Reserve judgment. Put your energy and attention into understanding fully what the other person is saying.
- Ask questions to encourage less talkative people to continue or to get more information.
- Be aware of biases you may have toward the speaker and work to overcome the effect these may have on your ability to really listen and understand that person. (For example, you may have difficulty listening to the person because of the way he or she talks, dresses, or looks; because of past difficulties you have had working with that person or that type of person; or because of your own racial, ethnic, religious, age, or other prejudices.)

The second step toward reaching consensus is to show understanding. Before giving your ideas or reacting to the other person's ideas, let him or her know that you understand those ideas. Briefly paraphrase what he or she has said; then pause to encourage a response. This technique will test whether you have truly understood what the other person said. Once you have listened to and understood the other person, you will have earned the right to share your ideas.

In fact, offering your ideas is the third step in the consensus-building process. But be sure to build on the other person's ideas. To increase your chance of being understood, state your ideas briefly and clearly. If you feel strongly about something, say so and give reasons why you believe the way you do. Pause and allow the other person to ask questions.

The fourth step is to work toward a solution that meets both people's needs. This step usually involves working through differences. You can often overcome clear differences of opinion by summarizing the two points of view and then aiming to build a solution that will satisfy you both. For example, you might say, "So what's important to you is to finish the Biltmore project before starting the Lincoln assignment. And what I need is to make some progress on the Lincoln assignment before the end of the quarter. Let's look for a way to satisfy us both."

In summary, here are the four steps you can use to reach consensus:

1. Draw out the other person's ideas.
2. Show understanding.
3. Offer your ideas.
4. Work toward a solution that meets both people's needs.

PROBLEM SOLVING ONE ON ONE

One-on-one problem solving addresses two types of problems: those that the employee "owns" and must solve single-handedly and those that the leader and employee must solve jointly.

Employee-Owned Problems

It has already been noted that one of the key roles of a facilitative leader is to help people solve their own problems. When someone comes to you with a problem that is clearly personal—a problem with managing his or her own time or getting along with another team member, for example—it is tempting to give advice. Telling people how to solve their problems is a natural instinct. However, people usually resist changing their ways. Your suggestions are likely to be refuted or ignored. You may hear phrases like "I wish I could, but..." or "That would probably work if only I didn't..." or "Every time I try that it doesn't work because...."

A healthier and more productive technique used by psychologists is also useful for managers and team leaders. The technique is to acknowledge the problem and get the person to see it as his or her own. Peck (1978, p. 32) emphasizes the importance of people's taking responsibility for their problems in this way: "We cannot solve life's problems except by solving them. We can only solve a problem when we say, "This is *my* problem and it's up to me to solve it."

An effective leader can help others take responsibility for their problems by helping them learn problem-solving techniques—not by solving the problems for them. Managers are often so intent on reaching goals that they cut the process short, coming up with solutions to the problems of others. What happens is a "Catch 22" situation, in which the manager tells a subordinate what to do to solve a problem, the subordinate resists the suggestion, the problem therefore remains, and the manager ends up having to step in and solve the problem.

A more effective approach is to acknowledge that the subordinate has a problem and to ask how he or she thinks the problem can be solved. For example, let us assume that Dan, one of your employees, has come to you with a problem. He is having trouble getting along with Sandy, with whom he is working on a project. Sandy has failed to meet her deadlines, putting Dan in a bind to meet his own goals. You believe this is a problem Dan can and should handle on his own. You say, "Dan, I agree with you. You do have a problem. What ideas do you have for working this thing out?" This approach accomplishes several things:

- You avoid taking on Dan's problem.

- You acknowledge Dan's problem and encourage him to act on it.
- You suggest that Dan already has some ideas about how to solve the problem.

The first step is to get Dan to agree that this is his problem and not someone else's. Until he accepts this responsibility, he is likely to resist taking action to solve the problem. Instead, he may continue to blame Sandy. Once Dan has accepted ownership of the problem, he is ready for your help in figuring out how to solve it. Remember that you are not solving the problem for him. You are simply giving him a process for solving it himself.

By using open-ended questions, you can guide another person through a step-by-step, problem-solving process. Most experts agree that about six key steps are involved in solving a problem. Here is one version:

1. Identify the problem or goal.
2. Generate alternative solutions.
3. Establish objective criteria.
4. Decide on a solution that best fits the criteria.
5. Proceed with the solution.
6. Evaluate the solution.

To help another person *identify the problem*, which is the first step, ask one or more of the following questions:

- What seems to be the problem?
- How do you see the problem?
- What seems to be causing the problem?
- If the problem were solved, what would happen?

If the person is struggling to set personal or professional goals, ask:

- What are you trying to achieve?
- Where do you want to end up?

During this first step, it is natural—and desirable—to let the person talk about his or her feelings relating to the problem.

People often cannot work on solving a problem until they have a chance to vent their feelings about it.

To get the person to move on to the second step and *generate alternative solutions*, say something like "You have identified the problem (or goal) as.... What are some possible solutions?" Suggest that the other person think of as many ways as possible to solve the problem or achieve the goal.

Then help the person move on to the third step, *establish objective criteria*, by asking "What, if any, stipulations do you want to put on your solution? What must your solution achieve? What would you like your solution to accomplish or not accomplish?" Some possible answers are:

- "I'd like the solution to decrease my hours at work, rather than increase them."
- "The solution must help me meet the deadlines on my two critical projects."
- "I don't want the quality of my work to suffer on my two critical projects."

Next, to lead the person to the fourth step, *decide on a solution that best fits the criteria*, ask, "Which of the solutions you discussed earlier will best meet these criteria?" There may be more than one. If so, ask which one best fits the criteria and is the least difficult to act on.

At this point, you have coached the other person through the first four steps of a six-step process. Notice that you have not told him or her what the solution to the problem is. You have guided the person through the four steps by asking questions and getting him or her to think through each step. Thus you can now point out that the person has identified his or her own solution, and you can ask if anything is impeding the fifth step, which is to *proceed with the solution*. Offer some support, if appropriate. For example, you might offer to check back with the person in a few days to see how the solution is going.

The sixth step in the process is to *evaluate the solution*. In a few days, you can ask the person, "How well did the solution work?" To the end, this process keeps you from misappropriating the problem and helps you facilitate the other person's finding a solution.

Problems Requiring Joint Resolution

The second type of problem addressed by one-to-one problem solving is the kind that you and another person must solve jointly. Both of you have enough at stake to be willing to work on a solution. Again, you can use the six-step problem-solving model. However, instead of getting the other person to solve the problem, you will offer your own ideas as well. As you move through each step, build consensus:

1. Seek the other person's ideas.
2. Show understanding.
3. Offer your ideas.
4. Work toward a solution that meets both people's needs.

To start the joint problem-solving process, you can ask, "How do you see the problem?" Show the other person that you understand his or her point of view: "I see then. You see the problem as...." Then offer your ideas about what you think the problem is, building on the other person's ideas when you can. "I agree with what you said about.... I see the problem as...." Build a definition of the problem from both people's viewpoints. Then move on to the next step, which is to generate alternative solutions. Once more, build consensus as you generate solutions: "What possible solutions do you see?" The remaining four steps in the problem-solving process unfold in similar fashion.

The consensus model is not meant to be so rigidly followed that it is counterproductive. Its main purpose is to remind you to *listen first,* to give subordinates an opportunity to speak up without interruption, and to show that you understand what they have said. When generating alternative solutions, for example, it may be more natural for both the manager and the employee to contribute ideas and to build on each other's ideas. The consensus model reminds more directive, controlling leaders to stop and listen, not to dominate the conversation. Following the model perfectly is not the object. The object is to build consensus by making certain that both people's ideas are taken into account.

CONSTRUCTIVE CONFRONTATION

From time to time you must bring up a problem to a subordinate or team member. If that problem has to do with his or her performance, a performance you would like to change, you are dealing with the need to confront. The word "confront" frequently connotes strong and negative feelings. Many people will avoid direct confrontation at all costs and will try all sorts of ways to deal with the problem indirectly. They may first avoid the problem or hint around at it. They may sneak it into the conversation so it will not be too offensive. They may get angry, be sarcastic, or find some way to get back at the other person. But none of these approaches works well.

As a facilitative leader, you can use a more constructive method for dealing with others' performance problems. First, be *direct* and to the point. If you have a problem, say so up front without camouflaging it. Second, be *specific* about what the problem is. State the facts as they relate to the specific problem. It helps to tell the other person what you expected would happen and explain what did happen from your viewpoint. Third, keep a *positive* and constructive tone and manner. Angry, accusatory behavior will alienate the other person, putting him or her on the defensive. Fourth, give the other person a *chance to respond* so you can begin to work out a solution. Ask, "What happened?" Remember to use an open, nonaccusatory tone of voice. Then pause and let the other person respond. Listen and do not interrupt. Ask questions to clarify what the other person has said.

Once you have brought the problem to the surface, you may need to explain why it is a problem. Tell the other person about the consequences of his or her behavior. Specify what you need from the other person. Determine what you will do and what the other person should do to resolve the problem. Determine the specific things that need to be done, specify when (time or date) they must be completed, and plan the next time you will get together.

Constructive confrontation avoids some of the common problems associated with confrontation. It deals with a specific here-and-now problem and does not blame others for a host of past problems. It does not assume that the other person is to blame; instead it gives the other person the benefit of the doubt. Asking "What happened?" gives the other person a chance to explain. You avoid attacking the other person while you are angry. Indeed, one of the main points to this approach is to avoid getting angry and blaming the other person. It is constructive, not destructive, because it builds toward a solution. The main point of the conversation is what went wrong and how you can both fix it, rather than who was wrong.

Part III

Facilitating Team Meetings

6

Meetings: The Heart of Teamwork

FUNCTIONS OF MEETINGS

Meetings are at the very heart of teamwork because of the important functions meetings perform. Much of what gets done in teams has a foundation in the group meeting. As is the case with democracy, meetings do not always work well, but they are the best way we have to get some things done. Those who live in the world of organizations know that these organizations are held together by face-to-face meetings.

Meetings fill a deep human need. Human beings are a social species. In every organization and every human culture that we have a record of, people come together in small groups at regular and frequent intervals and in larger gatherings from time to time. Meetings give people a sense of belonging to the group. Members of groups that do not meet regularly usually do not feel a strong sense of belonging and do not take ownership for the success of the group (Jay, 1968).

A meeting performs several key functions better than any other communication device. For one thing, meetings define the team, the group, or the unit. Those who are present belong; those who are absent do not. Meetings are where the group revises, updates, and adds to what it knows as a group. A group creates its own pool of shared knowledge,

67

experience, judgment, and folklore. As members exchange information and ideas they have acquired separately or in smaller groups, the group is strengthened. Meetings also help each member understand both the collective aim of the group and the way his or her own work, along with everyone else's, can contribute to the group's success.

Meetings are often the only time the team or group actually exists and works as a group and the only time when the leader, supervisor, or manager is actually perceived as the group leader. In meetings, the team's goals, direction, and norms for operating are established. Meetings create in all present a commitment to the decisions that the group makes and the objectives that the group pursues. Meetings are the forum for gaining consensus, solving group problems, and making group decisions. Once something has been decided, even if you argued against it, your membership in the group entails an obligation to accept the decision. The decision-making authority of a meeting is of special importance for carrying out key actions, policies, and procedures.

Meetings are an important reflection of how the group members work together. In the meeting arena, the team leader can find out how individual members relate to one another and to the group. People find out who they are in relation to the team. They find out how much they are listened to, whether their ideas are supported, and what their responsibilities are as group members. The team meeting is a key place to see the team in action.

For a team or department to function smoothly, it generally needs to have meetings on a regular basis. Well-functioning teams, however, do not necessarily need to have a lot of meetings to get their work done. In fact, the most effective teams do not always meet frequently. The meetings they do have, however, are productive and motivating.

Meetings, of course, serve functions besides those related to the group. Because of the complexity of organizations, goods, and services in American companies today, people simply must meet to share information and solve problems. The increased rate of change makes more meetings necessary. It is in the meeting setting where much information is shared, complexities are dealt with, misunderstandings are clarified, cross-functional issues and views are aired, and vital decisions are addressed.

It is becoming more important than ever for managers to have the skills and attitudes that make meetings productive. Issues that are not dealt with successfully in business meetings do not go away. *The meeting setting can be an efficient, productive, and beneficial way to get things done.* Unfortunately, many managers and team leaders are simply not skilled at leading a productive meeting. In addition to lacking skills, they may also have an inappropriate managerial style.

LEADERSHIP STYLE AND MEETINGS

Generally speaking, managers run their meetings the same way they manage people. Those who are autocratic and directive in their approach to managing will probably do most of the talking and controlling at their meetings. In contrast, more democratic and collaborative managers will probably listen more at meetings and draw out the opinions and ideas of their subordinates. Managers who tend to make up their minds before approaching others for an opinion may ask for the opinions of subordinates at meetings, but they will not pay much attention to those opinions. On the other hand, managers and team leaders who seek input from others before making a decision are more likely to listen during meetings.

Managerial meeting styles can be divided into these four categories:

- "Tell-'em, sell-'em" style;
- Information-dissemination style;
- Participative, "free-for-all" style; and
- Focused, participative style.

"Tell-'em, sell-'em" style. The manager comes to the meeting with his or her mind made up and explains the decision to the others. With force of personality and influential argument, this type of manager presents his or her ideas to subordinates, sometimes with forceful language and perhaps even passion. Meeting members are told how much their support is needed, and yet those members are given little opportunity to air their ideas, questions, or concerns. A few questions from subordinates may be answered throughout or at the end of the meeting, but little two-way communication is allowed.

Information-dissemination style. The manager uses meetings to inform everyone of what is going on in the department and in the larger organization. The manager, outsiders, and others in the department may give short or lengthy presentations to pass on vital (or not so vital) information. Meeting members may be given the opportunity to ask questions and discuss ideas, but the main focus of the meeting is the dissemination of information. Some people refer to these meetings as "information dumps."

Frequently, this type of meeting turns into an issue-raising session, during which all kinds of potential and real problems surface. But these problems are rarely resolved, because the meeting time is devoted to providing information. Meetings of this nature often become political platforms, where members vie for visibility and shoot holes in one another's information or projects.

Participative, free-for-all style. The manager gives meeting members more than ample time to participate and contribute. However, they make little progress toward solving problems or making decisions. This type of meeting is frustrating to those who need closure on issues or who need decisions made before they can progress with their projects. It is equally frustrating to those with busy schedules and under pressure to meet deadlines. Such a meeting seems like a waste of time.

Managers who use this style usually want input and participation from group members but lack the desire or skills to bring issues to closure. Managers of "participative free-for-alls" do not spell out clear objectives up front, and therefore consensus is difficult to reach in these meetings. The result: an interactive but meandering meeting where little is accomplished.

Focused, participative style. The manager encourages participation and involvement and focuses the group on clear meeting objectives. These objectives are agreed on by the group early in the meeting. This is the most desired style of meeting management if the meeting calls for group involvement and productivity. All group members become actively involved, and although the group may occasionally get off on a tangent, this type of manager soon refocuses the group on the defined objectives. This is the style of meeting leadership that this book addresses.

If managers and team leaders want support and commitment from people, they need to learn how to draw people out and collaborate with them both individually and collectively. To maximize their human resources, leaders need to bring out the experience and knowledge of everyone in the group, which a "focused, participative" approach can help them do. Managers who become more facilitative in meetings will undoubtedly take a more facilitative approach to managing in general.

WHAT GOES WRONG AT MEETINGS

"Not another meeting!" is a common lament in the hallowed halls of organizations today. The well-run, productive meeting seems to be the exception rather than the rule. In fact, so many things can go wrong at meetings, it is a wonder that some meetings do go well! Considering the amount of time wasted in meetings and their usual lack of productivity, it is surprising that such a small number of organizations focus on improving meetings.

In their studies of meeting management in America, Mosvick and Nelson (1987) found that the average manager and technical professional spend nearly a fourth of their total work week in meetings. According to Mosvick and Nelson, "Studies show that on average we spend more time in meetings of three or more people than in any other communication activity except one-to-one meetings" (p. 3).[6]

More startling than the amount of time spent in meetings is the fact that, as studies and surveys show, over 50 percent of the time spent in meetings is wasted. In other words, more than half of the meeting hours spent in America today are unproductive!

The low productivity rate of business meetings puts a tremendous drain on our productivity as a nation. Not only are we are losing billions of hours of precious time, a commodity that cannot be reproduced, but we are also spending billions of dollars unproductively. Those billions could be put to better use at a time when we are losing our competitive edge in many international markets.

Despite the problems with meetings, we are running more of them than ever. The accelerating rate of change in all aspects of business and government has created the need for ad-hoc meetings, cross-functional task forces, meetings with customers, team meetings, and ongoing staff meetings. Much of the time spent in these meetings is used to communicate, understand, and plan for change.

The need for productivity in meetings has never been so great. To compete successfully, American businesses must pursue all opportunities to save time and money. Because of

---

[6] From WE'VE GOT TO START MEETING LIKE THIS! by Roger K. Mosvick and Robert B. Nelson. Copyright © 1987 by Roger K. Mosvick and Robert B. Nelson. Reprinted by permission of Scott, Foresman Professional Books.

the vast resources poured into meetings, they are a fitting target for productivity improvement.

Numerous problems are commonly associated with meetings. Mosvick and Nelson (1987) surveyed 950 managers and technical professionals on meeting efficiency and came up with these top sixteen meeting problems, listed in order of importance:

- Getting off the subject;
- No goals or agenda;
- Too lengthy;
- Poor or inadequate preparation;
- Inconclusive;
- Disorganized;
- Ineffective leadership/lack of control;
- Irrelevance of information discussed;
- Time wasted during meetings;
- Starting late;
- Not effective for making decisions;
- Interruptions from within and without;
- Individuals dominate/aggrandize discussion;
- Rambling, redundant, or digressive discussion;
- No published results or follow-up actions; and
- No premeeting orientation/canceled or postponed meetings. (p. 19)[7]

At workshops on meeting facilitation that the author leads, participants identify what went wrong in meetings they have attended. Again and again, these same meeting problems—and others—come up. Most problems fall into four categories, all of which arise from unskilled, ineffective meeting leadership:

---

[7] From WE'VE GOT TO START MEETING LIKE THIS! by Roger K. Mosvick and Robert B. Nelson. Copyright © 1987 by Roger K. Mosvick and Robert B. Nelson. Reprinted by permission of Scott, Foresman Professional Books.

- No clear meeting objective or purpose;
- Ineffective meeting processes;
- No closure or follow-up; and
- Disorganization in planning or running the meeting.

THE RESULTS OF POOR MEETING LEADERSHIP

Several problems result from poor meeting leadership. Without a clear reason for meeting, it is natural for people to go off on tangents or for meeting time to be wasted on irrelevant discussion. Even if an agenda is published, it may not be enough to really focus the group on an objective or a meeting outcome. (Chapter 8 presents more on the problems with agendas and the importance of objectives.)

Without a clear meeting purpose, the leader will have trouble inviting the right people. Without a clear focus, people will be at the meeting for varying or unclear reasons. Their personal reasons will dominate, such as feelings of obligation, the desire for power and recognition, the need to address their own individual issues, or simply anxiety about being absent if something important is discussed.

Ineffective meeting processes also cause a host of problems. If participation is not structured and managed well, if conversation does not flow, and if people's ideas are not recorded and considered, the group will not be productive. A number of things can go wrong: Group members are interrupted or discounted by others, the leader dominates the discussion, not enough time is set aside for meaningful participation, conflict and disagreements do not get resolved, solutions are hastily arrived at with little reference to objective criteria. Decisions may be railroaded by dominant group members, with some people left out of the process altogether. No record of ideas is posted for use in discussing, planning, and deciding. Clarity and agreement about people's roles and responsibilities, or about the intended outcome of the meeting, are lacking. Any of these problems is enough to limit the meeting's effectiveness.

Without adequate meeting processes, the group is unlikely to achieve consensus or closure—even if it wants to do so. Closing on something that was not identified as a meeting objective in the first place is very difficult.

Once closure is reached—if it is—meeting leaders often fail to review exactly what was decided so everyone understands. Sometimes in the push to end the meeting, follow-up actions are overlooked. And even when follow-up is planned, it is not always acted on. Sometimes decisions are reached without giving proper authority to those who must carry them out. Or closure may be postponed to another meeting but never be addressed again.

Disorganization in planning and running the meeting is largely responsible for the bad reputation of meetings. Disorganization seems to be the norm, rather than the exception. Here are some typical manifestations of meeting disorganization:

- The meeting is called and then canceled or postponed, sometimes several times.
- The meeting is held when a memo or phone call would have sufficed.
- Premeeting communication is inadequate or confusing.
- The meeting room is inadequate: too large, too small, too noisy, lacking needed materials and equipment.
- Record keeping during the meeting is nonexistent, disorganized, or poor.
- The wrong people are present, and the right people are absent.
- The meeting leader arrives late, leaves early, or assigns someone else to lead who is not prepared.
- The meeting starts or ends late, time is wasted during the meeting, or the schedule is not adhered to.

Why do so many meetings seem to go nowhere? Why are most meetings a waste of everyone's time and effort?

Why do people seldom leave a meeting feeling that they have accomplished something? There are three main reasons: (1) The purpose of the meeting is not clear; (2) the meeting progresses in a rather jumbled, haphazard fashion (or consists of one presentation after another); and (3) the meeting ends with little consensus or commitment. In short, meetings tend to have fuzzy beginnings, directionless middles, and endings with no closure.

7

Leading
a Participative Meeting

WHAT MEETINGS NEED

To be productive, meetings need clear objectives, a defined process, and closure on the objectives. Generally speaking, a successful meeting accomplishes two things: (1) Something gets resolved, and (2) members leave the meeting committed to follow through on the decisions that are made.

The model for leading meetings is the same as the model for managing and leading teams:

Lead with objectives.

Empower to participate.

Aim for consensus.

Direct the process.

Lead with objectives. When clear meeting objectives are stated up front, the group's energy is directed toward achieving that outcome. The objectives then drive the *content* of the meeting. The facilitator must therefore see that the meeting begins with clear objectives. When team members are given, or help create, the objectives for the meeting, they are more able to contribute something of value and less likely to wander or be concerned with unrelated matters.

Empower to participate. To draw on the knowledge and experience of those present at a meeting, the leader must encourage active participation from all who are present. The L.E.A.D. model emphasizes participation and gives the leader responsibility for getting it.

Aim for consensus. For a meeting to be worthwhile, it must have an outcome, accomplish something. This is where consensus comes in. Without consensus and closure, a meeting has a feeling of futility; members leave wondering what they accomplished. Without the opportunity for consensus, members may feel either that nothing was accomplished or that they were railroaded into something on which they did not completely agree. A facilitator's ability to get a group to consensus is critical to the meeting's success. Through the process of consensus, members "sign up" to support and carry out the decisions of the team.

Direct the process. Just as important as clear objectives, participation, and consensus is the *process* of the meeting—how the meeting progresses. The process greatly influences the quality of the decisions made by the team. The meeting process also influences the commitment of each team member to the decisions made at the meeting. The L.E.A.D. model thus emphasizes the importance of process. However, many meeting leaders are so concerned with the meeting content that they ignore the process. For a meeting to be productive, it must involve all group members, encourage creativity and different viewpoints, and provide time for analyzing and solving difficult issues. A productive meeting needs a leader to guide its content, by helping the group set clear meeting objectives, encouraging a high level of involvement and participation, and leading the group to consensus and closure.

PROCESS VERSUS CONTENT

It is important for meeting leaders to know the difference between the *process* of the meeting and the *content* of the meeting. Content is what the meeting is about, the subject or issue
at hand; process is how the subject is dealt with. The content
is what people usually have the most opinions about: what
computer system to purchase, whether to redesign the product, what training program to implement, how to meet the
quarterly profit goal, and so on. Meeting processes include
discussions, presentations, premeeting committee or subgroup work, and flip charts used to record people's ideas. To
test your understanding of the difference between process
and content, take the quiz in Figure 5.

In most meetings, the process gets less attention than the
content. The process is generally governed by a set of company or organization norms about how meetings should proceed. Some companies, for example, rely heavily on overhead
slides and a presentation format. Others use flip charts with informal discussion. Some use a combination of both. One of the
first and most important things to remember is this:

The process (how the meeting proceeds) is as important
as the content (what the meeting is about).

If you refer to the list of things that go wrong at meetings (in
Chapter 6), you will see that the majority of problems stems
from ineffective meeting processes.

In summary, the content of a meeting is what the meeting is about; the process is the method used to get the work
of the meeting done.

FROM PRESENTATION TO FACILITATION

To understand more about meeting processes, think of a
presentation-facilitation continuum (see Figure 6). In pres-
entational meetings, the leader does most of the talking and

Indicate after each item below whether it represents the *content* or the *process* of a meeting:

	Content	Process
1. Statement of the problem	_____	_____
2. Group discussion of the problem	_____	_____
3. Information on a new procedure	_____	_____
4. Progress report	_____	_____
5. Breaking out into small groups to discuss the advantages and disadvantages of a suggested procedure	_____	_____
6. Idea contributed by one of the normally quieter group members	_____	_____
7. Several side conversations going on at once	_____	_____
8. Flip charts posted around the room with ideas the group generated		
a. The flip charts	_____	_____
b. The ideas	_____	_____
9. Three alternatives to organizing a staff	_____	_____
10. Brainstorming session	_____	_____

Note: Answers appear at the end of this chapter, on page 88.

Figure 5. Quiz on Process Versus Content

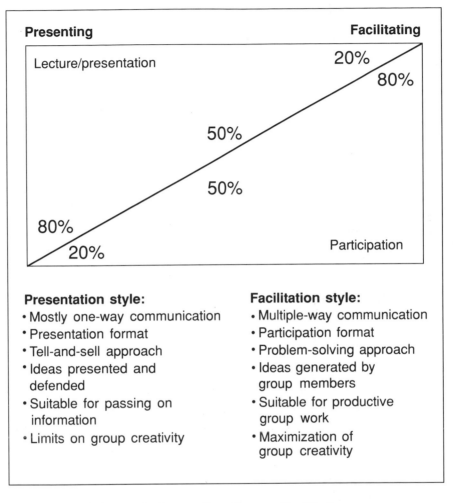

**Figure 6. Presenting Versus Facilitating:
Leadership Styles**

group members participate very little. In facilitated meetings, the leader does little of the talking and group members participate most of the time.

The presenting style is a form of one-way communication, in which information is passed from the meeting leader to those attending the meeting. This type of meeting can be useful if the goal is to tell, sell, advocate, explain, inform, or announce. But some people question whether this type of meeting should be held at all. Information can be passed on through the written word, making a meeting unnecessary. As Daniels (1986, p. 3) says, "The pure information dissemination meeting, held at regular periods during the work life of an organization, has one guaranteed result: boredom!" He recommends first and foremost that management "do everything possible to diminish the time spent in pure information dissemination. Getting people together solely for this purpose is to ask for failure" (p. 3).

Daniels has a second recommendation:

> Give the group work to do. The underlying assumption in calling any good meeting is that people are being brought together to do what groups do best: employ their members' minds in processing information for the purpose of problem solving, decision making, or planning. Information processed for these purposes is useful—never boring—and the process of using it is one of discovery and exhilaration. (p. 3)

In contrast to the presentation, the facilitated meeting requires the involvement of group members. The reasons for this type of meeting are to listen, discover, uncover or solve problems, decide, create, and plan. A facilitated meeting could also be called a working session, where tasks are tackled and results are achieved.

A leader's style of running meetings can fall anywhere along the presentation-facilitation continuum. However, too many meetings lean toward the presentation side of the continuum, and too few fall into the facilitation category. The best style is the one that suits the purpose of the meeting. If the purpose of the meeting is simply to inform the group and answer questions, the presentation style is adequate. If, however, a great deal of input from group members is needed and ongoing commitment is important, a facilitating approach works best (see Figure 7).

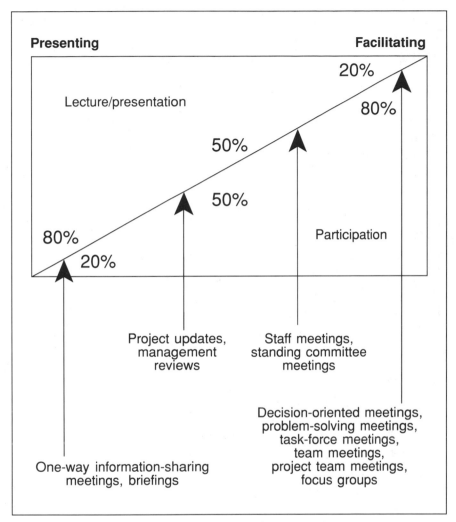

**Figure 7. Presenting Versus Facilitating:
Types of Meetings**

The meeting leader's responsibility for the content and out-come of the meeting is greater on the presentation side of the continuum than on the facilitation side. On the facilitation side, group members share responsibility for the meeting outcome. The facilitator, however, is neutral on the outcome of the meet-ing—although he or she takes great responsibility for the meeting process. Therefore, moving along the continuum from presentation to facilitation is sometimes difficult. Managers and group leaders often have a vested interest in the content of the meeting and have trouble remaining neutral.

ROLE OF THE MEETING FACILITATOR

A facilitator serves as a guide or a catalyst to help the group get its work done. The facilitator seeks not to give an opinion on the meeting *content* but simply to direct the *process* so the best work of the group gets done. The facilitator provides the method and structure for a group to focus its energy and creativity on a particular task.

Doyle and Straus (1976) describe the facilitator as "the neutral servant of the group." They explain that a facilitator is different from a mediator. Although the role of the facilitator is similar to the neutral, third-party role of mediators and arbitrators, there is a major difference: Mediators and arbitrators get involved in the content of a dispute. Doyle and Straus explain the difference in this way:

> The mediator acts like a diplomat, running back and forth between the two parties and making suggestions about what the final resolution should be. The arbitrator has power to act like a judge, and after listening to both sides, make a final decision. A facilitator remains detached and therefore more unbiased and neutral. He or she does not get involved in the content of the problem, but only in making suggestions about ways to reach solutions.... Even though the facilitator may have personal opinions about an issue, these opinions are not expressed (or allowed to interfere), which is why it's much easier to get all parties to agree to a facilitator than to a mediator or arbitrator. (pp. 80-81)[8]

---

[8] From *How to Make Meetings Work* by M. Doyle and D. Straus, 1976, New York: Jove Books. Reprinted by permission.

A facilitator must have knowledge of group processes and make certain that meeting participants are using the most efficient methods for accomplishing their task. When it comes to the content of the meeting, the facilitator remains nonevaluative.

Doyle and Straus describe the facilitator as a traffic cop directing the meeting's process. The facilitator provides rules or norms for the group and then monitors the group so it does not violate those norms. For example, if a group is brainstorming ideas to solve a problem, the facilitator may instruct the group that all ideas will be recorded and considered and that, in the initial stages of the brainstorming process, no one is to evaluate or discount any of the ideas. If someone tries to evaluate or discount an idea, the facilitator intervenes to remind the group of the rules.

A group that is used to being facilitated will begin to suggest its own processes and will police itself somewhat. However, groups that are new to facilitation need to be reminded from time to time about how to proceed.

One exception to the "rule" of remaining neutral on content is when a facilitator is conducting a training program or passing on important information. In these cases, the facilitator may play a dual role: content expert (presenter) and process expert (facilitator). A skilled trainer learns when to teach, or be the content expert, and when to step back and simply facilitate a discussion or group exercise. The facilitator-trainer judiciously chooses when to encourage the group to discover, discuss, and decide on its own. A facilitator-trainer can actually lead a training session without being the content expert, as long as there is someone present who can be a content resource.

There is really no right way to facilitate, no prescribed facilitator approach or style. Much depends on the facilitator's personality, the situation, the nature of individuals in the group, and certainly the dynamics of that particular combination of people. No two facilitations are alike, since the very nature of facilitation encourages ongoing adaptation to the group and to the task at hand.

Facilitators draw from a tool bag of techniques when planning and leading a meeting. Here are some of the things skilled facilitators do:

- Maintain a climate conducive to participating, listening, understanding, learning, and creating;
- Listen actively;
- Help the group establish and accomplish its own objectives;
- Provide structure and guidance to increase the likelihood that objectives will be accomplished;
- Keep the group focused on its objectives;
- Encourage dialog and interaction among participants;
- Suggest and direct processes that empower and mobilize the group to get its work done;
- Encourage the group to evaluate its own progress or development;
- Capitalize on differences among group members for the common good of the group;
- Remain neutral on content and be active in suggesting and directing the process;
- Protect group members and their ideas from being attacked or ignored;
- Use facilitation skills to tap the group's reservoir of knowledge, experience, and creativity;
- Sort, organize, and summarize group inputs or get the group to do so; and
- Help the group move to healthy consensus, define and commit to the next steps, and reach timely closure.

The objective, process-oriented role of the facilitator is critical. Someone needs to guide the process of the meeting. But facilitating and contributing to the meeting at the same time require concentrated effort.

Most people at a meeting, including the group leader or boss, are interested in the content or outcome and therefore have trouble being objective. Meeting members have a lot to do just to function as effective meeting participants. They must think through their ideas and express them so others will understand and consider them. They must hear and consider the ideas of others.

Meeting members may also have to deal with tensions resulting from "hidden agendas"—personal issues they may want to address. Some may be acutely aware of these agendas but may not feel comfortable addressing them. Others may not even be aware of their own hidden agendas, which nevertheless cloud the picture for them. Whether conscious or subconscious, hidden agendas often influence the meeting. They are usually expressed or dealt with in indirect—and often unhealthy—ways.

To further complicate the process, a meeting often becomes a place where people pursue interpersonal and political issues or vie for visibility. Most group members have trouble putting personal and political issues aside during a meeting. Someone needs to keep the group on track. The facilitator can help discover and then dilute or refocus hidden agendas. A skilled facilitator will balance such digressions with the group's objective.

The facilitator's role is to provide objectivity and identify and explain processes that will help the group get its work done. Must the facilitator therefore be someone from outside the group? Is it impossible for the manager or team leader to achieve this neutral role? Not necessarily. However, the facilitator must be someone who can—and will—remain neutral during the meeting, someone who will direct the process fairly. This is the challenge to the meeting leader: to be neutral, to empower others to get the work done.

To lead a participative meeting, managers and team leaders need the following skills:

- Designing and planning a meeting;

- Focusing the meeting;

- Encouraging participation;

- Recording people's ideas;
- Managing the group process;
- Organizing, connecting, and summarizing data; and
- Bringing the group to consensus and closure.

These skills will be covered in the next few chapters.

A facilitator should not only have these skills but also be able to present and develop a topic, since occasionally he or she needs to put on a "content hat" and explain something or pass on information.[9]

ANSWERS TO QUIZ IN FIGURE 5

Items 1, 3, 4, 8b, and 9 represent the *content* of a meeting; the rest represent the *process* of a meeting.

---

[9] In a well-organized and entertaining book entitled *Presentations Plus: David Peoples' Proven Techniques*, D.A. Peoples (1988) explains how to plan, develop, and deliver a good presentation.

8

Planning and Focusing
the Meeting

WHY AGENDAS DO NOT WORK
AND OBJECTIVES DO

Simply speaking, objectives are focused, agendas are not. Objectives define the desired outcome of the meeting; agendas define only the topics to be covered. Objectives give teams and groups something to strive for; agendas give them something to endure. Objectives call for active participation; agendas permit passivity.

Most people agree that one of the most important ingredients of a meeting is an "agenda" and that a meeting is successful if the agenda is adhered to and completed. Without a doubt, a meeting with an agenda that serves as a focal point is more successful than a meeting that rambles on and on without an agenda or a time schedule.

However, an agenda is not enough. It usually includes only a list of topics to be covered, a time schedule, and the name of the presenter for each item. A typical agenda might look like this:

9:00	Update on the Colby Project	Tom
9:30	The July 7-8 Offsite	Jean
10:00	Third-Quarter Report	Bob
10:30	Open Agenda	
11:00	Adjourn	

The dangers lurking in an agenda like this are many. First, it provides no clearly stated objectives for the meeting. What is the purpose of the meeting? For each agenda item, what will be accomplished? What do the members expect to accomplish? How will they know the meeting was successful? Because the desired outcome is not spelled out, the leader will have trouble keeping the group on track. When group members take off on tangents, the leader will have no stated purpose to bring them back to.

A second danger with agendas like the one above is that the topics it lists may not be the main concern of the group. Unless group members come up with the agenda, which does not usually happen, they are not likely to be very interested in it.

Third, using agendas and omitting objectives can lead to three unproductive developments:

- A series of long-winded, boring presentations;
- Several free-for-all discussions going nowhere; and
- A combination of boring presentations and free-for-all discussions.

A fourth problem with agendas is their excessive flexibility. A safe guess is that 50 percent or more of meetings with agendas never adhere to the set schedules. Agenda items are moved around, added, and deleted; people come and go; someone takes more than the allotted time; the group gets sidetracked or bogged down on one agenda item. Such a meeting suffers a sense of disorder and a loss of direction, and people feel that it will just go on and on with no defined stopping point.

The way to avoid such problems is to establish one or more clearly stated objectives for the meeting. An agenda can then be created to support the objectives. Instead of a list of topics, the agenda becomes a flow of activities that the team or group will take part in to accomplish the objective.

A sample meeting objective with its supporting agenda might look like this:

Our objective for today's meeting is to decide which one of the three alternative data-base management systems best meets our established criteria. The agenda for the meeting will be:

9:00	Review criteria. Make necessary changes.
9:30	Discuss pros and cons of each system in relation to criteria.
10:00	Plot decision grid. Rank choices.
10:30	Discuss top-ranked choice. Weigh against criteria. Decide on system.

Another way of publishing the agenda is to leave off the times, showing only the approximate length of the meeting:

Agenda
September 27, 1990
9:00-10:30

- Review criteria. Make necessary changes.
- Discuss pros and cons of each system in relation to criteria.
- Plot decision grid. Rank choices.
- Discuss and decide.

When managers and team leaders become comfortable with leaving decisions to the group and group members get used to facilitation processes, the objectives and agenda can be created by the group before the meeting begins. This practice is an excellent way to strengthen the group and increase the likelihood that the meeting will be productive. Everyone will have a say not only in the goal for the meeting but also in how the meeting will proceed.

OBJECTIVES: THE DRIVING FORCE OF A GOOD MEETING

Before calling a meeting, the most important question to ask is "What will this meeting achieve?" This question can be answered before the meeting by the leader, or it can be the first issue addressed at the meeting: "What do we need to accomplish at this meeting today?" "What would happen if we didn't have this meeting?" "When the meeting is over, how will we know it was successful?" Unless the need for the meeting is very clear, it may be a waste of everyone's time.

The meeting's objective leads to additional considerations:

- *Is the meeting necessary?* Can the objective be accomplished more efficiently in another way?

- *Who should attend the meeting?* Those who have information related to the objective or who will be involved in authorizing or implementing the objective need to be at the meeting. Others do not.

- *When should the meeting be held? How long do we need?* Both questions should be answered with the meeting objective in mind.

- *Where should the meeting be held?* What environment and atmosphere does the meeting call for?

- *Is any premeeting work necessary?* Will the group accomplish more if members prepare for the meeting ahead of time? What should members bring to the meeting?

- *What processes will accomplish the objective?* Brainstorming? A problem-solving model? Small-group work? An informative presentation? A short training session? Prioritizing?

- *What adjustments need to be made during the meeting?* As the meeting progresses, is the group making progress toward its objective, or does it need to do something different?

- *Was the meeting successful?* Did the group achieve what it set out to achieve? If not, why? How might the next meeting be improved?

Clear objectives are probably the most important element of a productive meeting. They help the leader to maintain control while encouraging maximum participation. Objectives focus the group, drive the outcome, and serve as a measure of performance and productivity.

Skilled facilitators have discovered that clarifying and posting meeting objectives early in the meeting is a powerful way to focus the group, get people involved, and direct the meeting toward consensus. Also, they have learned that the wording of the objectives is important: Objectives need to be clear, realistic, focused, and measurable. The wording *is* the objective.

WRITING MEETING OBJECTIVES

Writing out the objectives for a meeting helps everyone understand its purpose. When the objectives are also posted where they can be seen during the meeting, they keep the group focused.

It is helpful to think of a meeting objective as having three ingredients: an action, an outcome, and qualifiers (if necessary).

Actions that groups can accomplish in a meeting are described by such words as *plan, develop, decide, determine, generate, identify, recommend, list, prioritize, solve, resolve,* and the like. Start the objective with an action word that describes what the group will do during the meeting, something that can be observed. For example, you can specify whether a group is to list something or decide something or plan something.

Avoid using action words that are vague or that do not lend themselves to clear results. For example, you can say the objective is to discuss something, but simply discussing something at a meeting does not produce much of a result. Words like *discuss, understand, update,* and *explore* do not describe clear outcomes. Replace them with more results-oriented words. Instead of "Discuss the pros and cons of our new telephone system," try "Decide how to improve the use of our new telephone system." Instead of "Discuss how to improve customer service," try "Generate a list of ideas that will improve customer service and select the top two or three for immediate implementation."

Each of the suggested objectives has two key ingredients: an action and an outcome. The action describes what the members will be doing at the meeting. The outcome tells what the product or result of that action will be. For example, in "Decide how to improve the use of our new telephone system," the action is *decide.* The outcome is *how to improve the use of our new telephone system.* The other example, "Generate a list of ideas that will improve customer service and select the top two or three for immediate implementation," specifies two actions: *generate* and *select.* The outcome of the meeting will be two or three ideas that will be implemented immediately. When members leave the meeting, they will have made specific decisions about what they are going to do to improve customer service.

Compare these meeting objectives to the sort of vague agenda items that are more typical. The previous two objectives might have been phrased this way on an agenda: (1) discussion of the new telephone system and (2) how to improve our customer service.

Objectives usually need some additional words to put them in clear focus for the meeting. These words, called qualifiers, further describe the objective and set important parameters, such as time frames. For example, one of the previous objectives includes several qualifiers (noted here in italics): "Generate a list of ideas *that will improve customer service* and select *the top two or three for immediate implementation.*" These qualifiers specify that the ideas have to improve customer service, that the group has to select the top two or three (not just one and not all of them), and that the two or three ideas that are selected have to be implemented immediately. An objective does not necessarily need this many qualifiers, but the more qualifiers you include, the clearer and more focused the objective will be. A good question to ask is whether you have included enough qualifiers to focus the group.

In summary, remember that a meeting objective must have an action, an outcome, and the qualifiers necessary to focus the group. Check also to see that your objective describes a realistic accomplishment for that meeting.

MANAGING MEETING FLOW

Once the meeting objectives have been decided and agreed on, the next step is to decide on the flow of meeting activities. This flow could be called the meeting "agenda." Figuring out how to lay out the meeting becomes easier with experience as a facilitator. An understanding of group process is important. What activity will get the group rolling? What is the best process to use to accomplish the objective? (Several processes for getting groups to come to consensus are described in Chapter 12.) Getting active participation and involvement is one skill; planning and structuring the meeting so participation will be productive is another.

The first step is to decide how you will focus the group on the purpose of the meeting. (Several ways to get a meeting focused are presented later in this chapter). The second step is to find a way to get everyone participating as soon as possible (see Chapter 9). One technique is to have some kind of introductory activity that will require everyone's input, so dominant members will not take over right at the beginning of the meeting. The third step is to plan the group processes you will use to accomplish the objective (Chapter 12 describes several, such as brainstorming and clustering). Finally, plan how you will close the meeting. What activity will you use to reach closure and to decide on the next steps the group must take? The meeting should not end until group members feel they can support the group's decision, clearly understand just what that decision is, and identify action steps and responsibilities for carrying out that decision.

When planning a meeting, remember that participation takes time. Leave plenty of time for each activity, and anticipate more discussion and involvement rather than less. Build in time for letting the group stray off the topic a bit, as digressions sometimes help people get a grip on the real problem. In the long run, time spent ensuring participation saves time. People will leave the meeting with more commitment to the group's decision and a clearer picture of what needs to be done.

PLANNING FOR PARTICIPATION

Here are some things to remember when planning a meeting:

- Start with an activity that includes everyone. Choose something easy for people to do or talk about, something that relates to the work at hand.
- If presentations are necessary, keep them short and to the point. Give people ample time following each presentation to comment and ask questions.
- Try to structure meetings so group members are talking 80 to 90 percent of the time. The leader-facilitator should listen, record, and suggest processes. Team members should do the thinking, talking, deciding, and so on.
- Vary activities to include some small-group or subgroup work. Let people work in pairs or in subgroups of three or four and then come back to the larger group to share their ideas or report their findings.

Avoid subgroup work, however, at the beginning and end of the meeting. Generally, it is best to start and end with all group members together.

- Decide before the meeting how you will organize data on flip charts or other media. Think ahead about problems that may arise in organizing the data and how you might deal with them. For example, if you are going to do brainstorming, the group will probably come up with a long list of ideas. You may want to leave a space before each idea so you can label it later.

- Anticipate that stray issues will come up, and decide ahead of time how you will handle them. One way is to appoint someone at the beginning of the meeting to record these ideas and bring them to the next meeting. Another way is to have a flip chart available so you can record the ideas as they come up. You can consult the group members at the end of the meeting about how they want to handle the extra ideas.

Chapter 9 presents some additional methods for fostering participation.

PREPARING NOTIFICATION MEMOS AND PREWORK

When planning the meeting, ask yourself what group members can do prior to the meeting to make it more productive. The tasks you come up with constitute the meeting prework. Caution: Prework that group members consider too time consuming, unclear, or unimportant probably will not get done. When planning the meeting, you must therefore also ask, "How likely is it that people will complete the prework? Is the prework really necessary?"

A group that meets regularly may not need a premeeting notification memo. The members may have agreed on

the prework and meeting objectives at the end of the previous meeting. But when a notification memo does need to
be distributed, use the opportunity to clearly state the objectives for the meeting. If the group is going to decide its own
objectives at the beginning of the meeting, the premeeting
memo might read, "We will start by determining what we
want to accomplish during the meeting."

FOCUSING A MEETING

The most productive groups clearly understand why they
are meeting and what they must accomplish. There are several ways to help group members focus on their objective:

- Use the *premeeting memo* to communicate the meeting
  objectives and let people know what to expect.
- Read and post the *objectives* at the meeting for all to
  see and refer to. If the group participates in creating
  its objectives for the meeting, write and post these objectives after the group has finalized them.
- Use the meeting *agenda* to let people know what activities to expect and about how long each will take.
  Then they can spend more energy participating and
  less energy wondering what is going to happen next
  or when the meeting will be over.
- At the beginning of the meeting, use an *activity that includes everyone.* Such an activity will reinforce the idea
  that everyone's contribution is valued and will help
  get everyone focused on the meeting.
- When appropriate, set *general rules or norms* for the
  meeting. The roles people will play in the meeting
  may also need to be defined. For example, will the
  group's leader be a participant in the meeting or the
  facilitator? Who will record the group's ideas and
  decisions? What role will guests or others play? Ex-
  plicit rules and roles are especially helpful if those at-

tending the meeting are not used to meeting to-gether or if the way the group has been operating is changing.

- Sometimes it is appropriate and valuable to ascertain the *expectations of group members* at the beginning. The facilitator then knows where people are coming from and can either adjust the meeting to meet their expectations or clarify up front that it will not be possible to meet them. One technique that works is to ask "Given our objectives for today, what expectations do you have for this meeting?" Give everyone a chance to think and respond, and record the comments; after all expectations have been expressed, address each one briefly. This technique helps people understand the intent of the meeting and focus on the objective at hand. It is especially useful for long, difficult meetings and meetings to which people are likely to bring a lot of issues, concerns, and hidden agendas.

Use these techniques to focus your meetings, and they will become more participative and productive.

9

Encouraging Participation

VERBAL TECHNIQUES: WHAT TO SAY

One of the facilitator's key roles is to create an atmosphere of openness and trust, to get people to speak up and contribute. Several techniques will either encourage or discourage participation in a group setting. Facilitators need to be keenly aware of what these are and use them appropriately to get a balance of participation. They include what the facilitator says, what the facilitator does, how the facilitator listens, how the activities are structured, and the room environment and setup. What the facilitator says can be referred to as verbal techniques; what the facilitator does can be referred to as nonverbal techniques. These verbal and nonverbal techniques are critical to being a good facilitator.

These are some of the most important verbal techniques:

- Ask open-ended questions.
- Phrase requests to encourage more responses.
- Acknowledge and positively respond to contributions made by participants.
- Ask for more specifics or examples.
- Redirect questions or comments to other members of the group.
- Encourage nonvocal participants to participate.
- Ask for and encourage different points of view.
- Paraphrase for clarity and understanding.

- Avoid stating your opinion or interjecting your own ideas while facilitating.
- Refer to contributions people have made.

Asking an open-ended question. Asking people a question that cannot be answered with "yes" or "no" is one of the easiest, most basic techniques for drawing people out. An open-ended question simply asks for information, an idea, a reaction, or an opinion. Open-ended questions usually begin with *"What," "How," "Who,"* or *"Why."* Some examples are:

- "What is your reaction to that?"
- "What, in your opinion, is the best way to...?"
- "What suggestions do you have to improve the way we...?"
- "How can we improve the way we handle customer complaints?"
- "What alternatives do we have?"
- "Why do you think we are having problems with...?"

Closed-ended, or directive, questions are those that can be answered with "yes" or "no" or that direct the respondent to specific answers. They begin with such phrases as *"Do you," "Are you," "Is that," "Does that,"* and *"Isn't it better to."* This type of question is useful in certain situations but not very effective for drawing on the synergy and expertise of a group. A good facilitator usually avoids closed-ended questions. They are effective, however, if the facilitator wants to wrap up a topic and move on. They also help get people to agree on specifics: "Are we in agreement, then, that...?" "Then is this the best alternative?"

Using requests to encourage more responses. Another important facilitator technique for encouraging participation is to ask people to supply more information or to expand on an idea. These types of requests usually begin with words or phrases like *"Describe," "Tell us,"* and *"Explain."* Here are some examples:

- "Describe the process you used."

- "Tell us more about that."

- "Explain the difference between the two systems."

Positively responding to contributions made by participants. A little positive reinforcement goes a long way; it can be overdone. The trick is to be genuine without being repetitious or distracting. Without any positive reinforcement at all, however, especially if the meeting leader appears serious and determined, meeting participants may not feel encouraged to open up or to speak their minds.

Positive reinforcement can be accomplished with such comments as *"Thank you," "Good point," "That's a new idea," "That's interesting,"* or *"Let's get that down."* To build rapport and personalize the meeting, it also helps to occasionally use the name of the participant: "Thank you for bringing that out, Jim" or "Thank you, Sue; that's a point we hadn't considered yet."

A word of caution is appropriate here. Using this technique too frequently lessens its effect. A facilitator should not comment after every input but just often enough to encourage people to contribute. The facilitator needs to strike a balance between being unresponsive and being overly responsive.

Other ways to positively reinforce contributions are discussed in this chapter under "Nonverbal Techniques: What to Do."

Asking for more specifics or examples. When open-ended questions and comments that encourage more responses do not bring out enough specifics, or when someone uses platitudes or generalizations that do not further people's understanding of the topic, the facilitator can move the discussion along by asking for specifics:

- "Could you be a bit more specific?"

- "Can you go further into that?"

- "What do you mean by...?"

- "Can you help us out by giving an example?"

Redirecting questions or comments to other members of the group. This powerful and much-underused technique encourages dialog among participants and draws attention away from the facilitator. For example, when asked a question by one of the participants, the facilitator might say something like "What do the rest of you think about that?" or "Someone here must have a response to that" or "I'd like to throw that question out to the whole group; what do some of you think?" Another appropriate use of this technique is when a group member comments on something said earlier by another member. The facilitator may then say something like "That relates to something Jim said earlier about.... Jim, what is your response?"

Although at times participants might find this technique annoying, redirecting questions or comments at the appropriate time puts responsibility for the discussion on the participants' shoulders, not on the meeting leader's. It also keeps the dialog going and knits participants together as a team. The leader who uses it is maintaining a balance of participation and ensuring that the team members respect and build on one another's ideas. Once group members get used to this technique, they may respond on their own if the facilitator just remains silent. Eventually they will direct their comments to one another instead of to the facilitator.

Encouraging nonvocal participants to participate. It is important to try to balance participation by drawing out even the quietest group members. The key is for the facilitator to be aware of who is participating and who is not. Someone who has not contributed may then be drawn out in a direct way: "Bill, any reaction to this?" or "Joan, we haven't heard from you yet; what do you think?"

If you suspect that the person's mind has wandered and that he or she may be caught by surprise, repeat enough of the topic to enable the person to respond. For example: "Sue, it's been a while since we heard from you. What do you think of the XYZ alternative?"

Another technique is to ask each person separately for a response to the same question. Used sparingly, this is a fine way to balance participation. Frequently, the quieter person is shy or does not want to interrupt others or is uncertain about when to jump in. In some cultures, like the Japanese culture, it is considered rude to interrupt another person. But in many American meetings, the talking does not stop long enough for someone to contribute in a "polite" way. As a result, Japanese often appear quiet even though they have contributions to make. A knowledgeable and sensitive facilitator will find ways to give people from all cultures the opportunity to speak up.

Asking for and encouraging different points of view. When group members are all in agreement and no different viewpoints have been expressed, several things may be wrong. Some people may be holding back for fear of recrimination. Or the group may be intent on coming to a quick solution so it can get on with other things. People who have been together as a team for some time may also start to think alike. This phenomenon, called "groupthink," inhibits creative problem solving. Of course, another possible reason for a lack of disagreement is that there really is little disagreement.

Lack of divergent viewpoints is a signal to the facilitator to intervene. When a group seems ready to agree before sufficient testing or development of ideas has taken place, the facilitator must open up additional discussion and consideration: "We have discussed only one or two viewpoints. Are there some other points of view on this subject?" or "Is there something we haven't thought of?" or "Can anyone think of a way this doesn't fit?"

If no one responds, the facilitator can try switching positions, throwing out a different view for consideration: "What about the view that...?" Facilitators should use this technique sparingly, because switching positions too often may make them appear too involved in the content or even manipulative. This technique should be used to help, not hinder, the productive work of the group. Fortunately, a group that is used to being facilitated will not need this technique very often.

Paraphrasing for clarity and understanding. This is a good technique for facilitators who want to check their understanding of what another person has said or who want to make sure that everyone in the room has a clear idea of what is being said. For example: "Let's see, Pete. If I understand correctly, you are saying...."

Avoiding stating your opinion or interjecting your own ideas while facilitating. Paraphrasing too frequently can be risky, especially if it gives group members the impression that you are rephrasing comments to make them sound better or to have the last word yourself. Participants will become demoralized if they get the message that their words are not good enough or if they feel that the discussion centers too much around the facilitator. Yielding to the temptation to comment on the proceedings discourages valuable interaction among the other participants, causing good thoughts to be lost and time to be wasted.

Referring to contributions people have made. When doing so will help the group be clear about its work, the facilitator may wish to relate one person's comment to another. For example, when two or three people are saying similar things, the facilitator may point out, "That sounds like what Yoshi said earlier about...." Cross-references like these help the group reach consensus. They also encourage and reward participation, showing that the facilitator is really listening to what people are saying.

NONVERBAL TECHNIQUES: WHAT TO DO

Although harder to pinpoint than verbal techniques, nonverbal techniques (what a facilitator does) are just as important.

In fact, what you do when facilitating must match what you say. If it does not, you will give mixed messages and create an atmosphere of distrust. For example, if you ask an open-ended question but move right into your next sentence without waiting for an answer, you are telling people you do not really expect them to respond. They will get the message that you do not want their contributions, and they will stop participating.

Your nonverbal behavior can let participants know that you are attentive, interested in their ideas, and willing to let them proceed without your interference. Some important nonverbal behaviors are these:

- Attentiveness;
- Voice and facial expressions;
- Silence; and
- Movement and position in the room.

Attentiveness. The most important rule of facilitation is to pay attention to the person who is talking. A facilitator who does not listen well hinders the group's productivity. Establishing good eye contact with the person speaking, relaxing your posture, and turning toward the speaker are all good ways to foster attention. A few head nods to show understanding will encourage the speaker to continue. Unless you need to cut off a long-winded person, you should not interrupt. Also avoid distracting movements (rattling keys, playing with a pen, and so on) and doing other things while people are speaking. One possible exception is writing the group's ideas on a newsprint flip chart. Although turning away to write on a flip chart may seem to detract from attentiveness, the act of recording someone's idea is usually powerful enough to make up for the loss of eye contact.

Voice and facial expressions. These may also enhance or detract from a facilitator's effectiveness. A voice that encourages participation is clear but not overpowering; it displays confidence and enthusiasm. The volume of the voice is loud enough for all to hear, projecting to the back of the room. Facial expressions similarly affect the mood of the group. A serious or deadpan face may bring down its energy level. Frowns tend to discourage participation. Smiles usually encourage and relax people, but too much smiling may discredit the facilitator and distract participants.

Silence. Because we are so often concerned with what we say, we may neglect what we do not say. Silence is a critical tool of a good facilitator and a much-forgotten art. Good listeners know when to pause, wait, and say nothing, and they regularly put this knowledge to use. It is especially important to pause after asking a question. Give people time to think of their responses; your pause will indicate that you really want to hear what they have to say. Try not to get anxious and restate or rephrase the question. A good rule of thumb is to wait about ten to twelve seconds. (Usually someone will respond after seven to ten seconds.) Those seconds will seem like a long time to you, but they will pass quickly for the people who are thinking about possible responses. If nobody responds after ten to twelve seconds, then ask the question again, rephrase it, or move on.

Using silence wisely makes the group responsible for its own progress. After someone has responded to one of your questions, be silent so participants can respond to one another; let the group carry on by itself. Above all, do not always insist on having the last word. You do not want to be the focal point; you want the others to interact.

Movement and position in the room. The way the facilitator moves around the room can affect participation. Generally speaking, standing fixed in one spot with hands and arms rigidly in some position (straight down, folded, or in pockets) is not a good idea. Stiffness conveys tenseness and nervousness. It is better to move about in a relaxed manner or to sit down than it is to stand in one spot. If the chairs in the room are arranged in a U-shaped configuration, you might occasionally move closer to the participants who are sitting at the base of the U. Moving closer to people naturally draws them into the conversation. Another technique is to move behind the participants, to the back of the room outside the U, and let the group carry on by itself. Use this technique after you have gotten a discussion started. Sitting down where you can see group members but they cannot see you also works well. Sometimes sitting down and joining the group works, but other times you may lose control of the group or lose your credibility. Sitting down for too long may also cause the group to be too relaxed and lose energy. This technique usually works best when the team is engaged in active discussion and the members have a lot of energy and enthusiasm for their topic.

MANAGING THE ENVIRONMENT

Some room environments discourage participation, so whenever possible set up the room to encourage dialog and interaction. Arrange tables and chairs so people can see one another. Position the flip chart and the overhead projection screen so they are visible to everyone. If you will be posting sheets of newsprint from a flip chart, make sure you have adequate room to hang them where people can see them.

Room layouts that are U-shaped or modifications of that shape are best (see Figure 8). Everyone can see almost everyone else and the visuals at the front of the room. The facilitator can stand, sit, or move in and out of the U. A conference table setup is second best. Group members can still see one another, but the facilitator and the visuals may not be so visible to everyone at the table. Refreshments are best placed at the back of the room; they become distracting when placed at the front of the room.

A meeting room should have adequate space, but participants should not feel dwarfed. For example, members of a new team meeting for the first time in a large conference

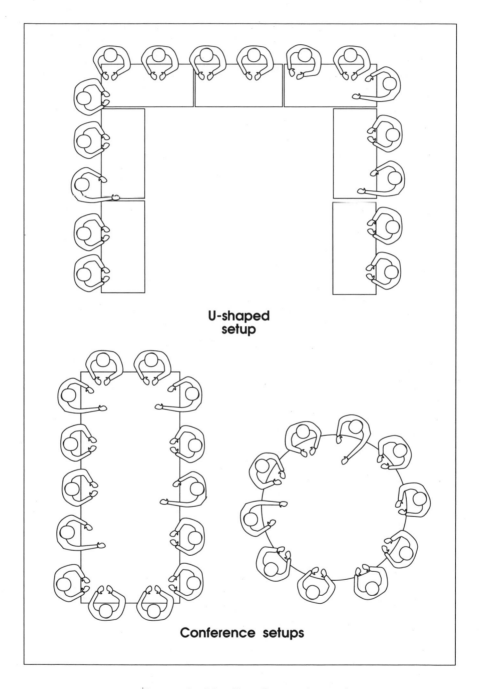

U-shaped setup

Conference setups

Figure 8. Meeting-Room Layouts

room may feel small and insignificant in such a large space. They may not participate as much as they would in a smaller room. If you must use a large room, try blocking off a smaller space with a screen, charts, or other barriers to create the feeling of a more intimate space.

For meetings that call for small groups to go off and work together, breakout rooms or spaces are important. They give small groups privacy and quiet and also give people a change of scenery. In fact, a change of scenery is a desirable break in any long meeting. Let people move around or work in a different area. If you cannot let them change rooms, assemble them into subgroups or pairs within the room.

Other considerations for choosing a meeting room are temperature, air, noise, and view. Aim to minimize distractions, discomfort, and disharmony. Stuffy rooms cause sleepiness. Rooms that are too cold or too hot make people uncomfortable. Windows bring cheer and openness to a room, although a distracting view reduces the group's productivity. Be aware of noise that interferes with the group's work, and try to control it as much as possible. It is better to stop the meeting and take time to reduce the noise than to try to carry on over the distraction.

GETTING INVOLVEMENT EARLY

The earliest stages of a meeting affect the level of participation later. Find an introductory activity that involves everyone during the first few minutes to let people know you really do want to hear from everyone. Make people feel involved right from the start. A few suggestions follow.

When people do not know one another, begin by having each person introduce himself or herself. List on newsprint a few things you would like each person to tell the group—anything that may help people work better together. Examples are:

- Name;
- Current position;
- Prior career or job;
- Other team experience;
- Expectations and hopes for this team;
- Reasons for choosing this team;
- Pet peeve about teams;
- Favorite vacation spot; and
- A favorite food.

Including something personal helps people relax, get better acquainted, and find things they have in common.

When holding the first meeting of a newly formed team or when starting a session that will emphasize teamwork, ask people to recall their first team experiences. After giving people some time to think, have each person tell the group:

- What type of team it was;
- When and where he or she was on the team;
- What his or her role on the team was;
- Positive or negative memories of being on the team; and
- What he or she learned about teams and being a team member from that experience.

While people are speaking about their team experiences, record some of the ideas. Here are some thoughts about teams that might be aired:

- The team was close-knit.
- We accomplished a lot.
- It was hard work.
- We had fun!
- We were somewhat autonomous.
- Our leader was demanding but fair.
- Other work suffered.
- We had enthusiasm and energy.

Later, summarize what the group said, emphasizing any points you wish to make about what makes a good team.

If you are working with a team whose members have been together for a while, ask each person to say a few words about what has happened since the last meeting that might affect the team's work. Jot down key points on a newsprint flip chart. Save this information and incorporate it into the meeting. If one or more people missed the last meeting, ask those who were present to suggest five words that describe that meeting. Write each word on a sheet of newsprint. Then have someone tell the absentees why those words were used to describe the meeting and to summarize what went on at the last meeting. Ask the rest of the group members if they have anything to add or change. Use their remarks to lead into your objective for the day. This activity gets everyone thinking about the last meeting, relaxes the group (and may even get a few laughs), brings the absentees up to date, and kicks off the current meeting.

The reason for undertaking an involvement activity at the beginning of the meeting is to balance participation right away and to establish the norm that everyone will be included. Daniels (1986, p. 16) says it this way: "Whatever is done during the first five minutes of a meeting establishes the norm state.... Providing an inclusion activity is the easiest and best way to deliberately shape the norm state into one of equal influence." The goal is to give everyone a chance to influence the outcome of the meeting. Meetings that begin with a long-winded presentation quickly lose participants' attention and make it less likely that they will get involved.

10

Recording and Posting
People's Ideas

THE POWER AND PURPOSE
OF RECORDING IDEAS

In traditionally run meetings, a secretary records the meeting minutes, and they are read or distributed at a later date. Recording ideas in a participative meeting takes a different form and has a different purpose. A newsprint flip chart, displayed on an easel, is the most common medium used for recording ideas. The completed sheets of newsprint become the working papers of a group in action. They contain ideas, data, opinions, alternatives, pros and cons, and issues that group members must consult as the meeting proceeds. When the group reaches consensus, the decision is written down— for all to see and agree on. Action items, time frames, and responsible parties are published then and there.

Possibly the most powerful argument for recording people's ideas is that it gives everyone a equal chance to influence and participate. Recording a person's idea, for all to see, acknowledges its value. The person who has thus contributed can then relax and listen to what others say or can think about others' contributions. The recorded idea is separated from the originator and later can be evaluated more objectively, on its own merits.

Recording people's contributions also allows recall of those ideas. Recorded ideas are the team's notes; they become the group's memory, a data bank for reference as the meeting proceeds. When a meeting is in progress, many thoughts and ideas are put forth. People become overwhelmed and confused, and each one ends up remembering mostly what he or she considers important. When concentrating on their own ideas and how to express them, people do not hear or remember what others say. Or they may remember only part of a point. But when the ideas are posted around the room, people are free to refer to what has already been said.

Studies show that we remember only a small percentage of what we hear (some say as little as 20 percent). Yet we remember a much larger portion of what we both hear and see (some say as much as 50 percent). Other studies prove that people—including the meeting leader—remember less than half of what was actually decided at a meeting. Recording meeting data and decisions is therefore critical if a team is to be productive.

The information that is recorded also serves as a record of the group's progress. It is sometimes difficult to know where the group is on a topic or task. Referring to information on newsprint can bring the group back from a tangent and keep everyone focused.

Keeping people from repeating the same things over and over again saves time too. The facilitator can discourage someone from bringing up a pet peeve repeatedly: "See, we have that recorded already" or "Is that the same as what Al said earlier?" When the group as a whole keeps covering the same territory again and again, the facilitator can move people on by saying, "Yes, that's a point we've written down. Let's move on to...."

WHY USE NEWSPRINT FLIP CHARTS?

Even if you are dead set against using flip charts, please read on and at least circle the things that make sense to you. Then—if you are still determined not to use flip charts—try to find another way to accomplish what flip charts do so well. You may wish to start using them on a limited basis until you feel comfortable with them.

A flip chart is one of the facilitator's most valuable tools. It serves as a physical focus for the group, a place to direct everyone's attention and energy. Completed sheets of newsprint are the group's common notes, and as such they draw team members together in a combined, synergistic effort. Transparencies do not work so well, since the group can view only one of them at a time. If you must use transparencies, however, stop every half-hour or so and have them copied, so everyone has a working copy to look at. This method creates a problem that flip charts do not have: Everyone focuses on his or her own copies, and the cohesiveness generated by using a common set of newsprint sheets is lost.

Flip charts do create problems, however, that must be taken into account when planning a meeting. Here are some of the problems that people have pointed out:

- Using them may go against company culture.
- They are cumbersome and require extra effort to set up and use. (A flip chart works best when it is set up on an easel, and easels are heavy and unwieldy.)
- The individual newsprint sheets are difficult to tear off and post. (Masking tape must be available for posting.)
- "I can't write legibly or large enough."
- The felt-tipped markers may dry up.
- "I can't listen, pay attention, and write all at the same time. A flip chart forces me to turn my back to people."
- Newsprint sheets are difficult to copy, store, and reuse.

With all these disadvantages, why bother with flip charts? No other effective means is available for quickly recording and posting people's ideas for immediate use in a meeting. Perhaps a less cumbersome method will be devised someday, but until then flip charts remain a critically important tool for facilitators.

THE ROLE OF THE RECORDER

Either the facilitator or someone else may actually do the writing on flip charts. Many fine facilitators prefer to do their own recording. However, a facilitator who has trouble writing on a flip chart or summarizing people's comments should probably ask someone else to serve as recorder. The position of recorder can also be rotated so everyone has a chance to participate in the meeting.

Whoever does the recording must be able to accurately capture people's ideas. He or she must listen carefully for the meaning of each idea and be careful not to leave out any ideas. If an idea closely resembles one that has already been recorded, the recorder can ask the participant if his or her comment is the same as the previous one. If the two ideas differ at all, even slightly, they should be recorded separately.

To remain neutral, the recorder must avoid jumping in with his or her own opinions or ideas. Participants will be annoyed if the recorder uses this central position to editorialize, add personal touches, or disagree with ideas being presented.

When someone else serves as the recorder, the facilitator needs to make sure all inputs are being accurately represented. Sometimes it is up to the facilitator to slow down the comments so the recorder has time to capture them or to coach the recorder on the wording of an idea.

HOW TO RECORD IDEAS

The most difficult part of recording is to accurately capture an idea in a brief phrase. The challenge is to record a key word or phrase while using the participant's wording as much as possible. At times you may have to ask the participant to restate the idea in a few words. Taking too much liberty in paraphrasing may change the meaning. Thus it is better to select a few words used by the participant than to reword what was said.

While a participant is talking, listen attentively to everything, looking for a key phrase that will summarize the statement. Give people time to ramble a bit, to wrestle with their thoughts. Seldom do people come forth with brief, well-stated ideas when difficult subjects are being discussed. Also, if you try to write everything, you will run out of newsprint, markers, time, and stamina. When you think you have singled out the main idea, write what you think best captures the thought. If you are not certain you have phrased the idea correctly, check with the speaker: "Does this capture what you said?" Sometimes you will not be able to get the main idea because the speaker is unclear, rambles, or states several ideas at once. Say something like "Can you summarize your idea in a phrase or two so I can record it here?"

ORGANIZING THE IDEAS

A participative meeting can produce a lot of data. Several newsprint sheets may be filled while group members discuss a question or brainstorm. Organizing the ideas that are recorded helps make them more accessible and useful.

To organize the ideas, you might first mark the beginning of each new one with a dash, a star, or a "bullet" (a large dot preceding an item). You could also number or letter each idea, especially if you think you will want to refer to

them several times or categorize them for further consideration. For example, in a brainstorming session about purchas-
ing new software, the following ideas might come up:

1. Replace the old software with Magi-Word.
2. Use both the old and the new software for a time and
   then evaluate.
3. Test Magi-Word by having 25 percent of the department use it first.
4. List our current and future needs and then evaluate
   both pieces of software.

Later, when the group is evaluating the ideas, each idea can
be referred to by its number.

Some facilitators like to use two colors of felt-tipped
markers. One color is used for the question, another for responses. Or colors are alternated as ideas are recorded, so
people can more easily determine where one idea leaves off
and another begins. Some facilitators write all the ideas in
one color and use a second color to circle or underline key
words when the ideas are being discussed or evaluated.

During a lengthy meeting, changing colors for each
new portion of the meeting may help later, when the group
is reviewing its work, reaching consensus, or planning follow-up. Changing colors is not necessary in this situation,
however; the facilitator or recorder can number each chart
as the meeting proceeds and post the charts in order
throughout the meeting. Numbering the charts also helps
later if the data are transcribed.

CREATING AND WRITING ON NEWSPRINT

The best resource for someone who wants to use flip charts
effectively is Brandt's (1986) *Flip Charts: How to Draw Them*

and How to Use Them.[10] In this informative and well-illustrated book, the author explains how to lay out flip-chart posters, how to print them, and how to choose effective color combinations. His samples illustrate how effective simple graphics can be.

When using a flip chart during a meeting, you will find that your newsprint sheets are messier than those prepared ahead of time. However, some general principles apply to creating newsprint sheets, regardless of whether the sheets are prepared ahead of time or during the meeting.

First, mind your handwriting. Write large and legibly so everyone can read what you have written. It is usually best to print, using either all capital letters or a combination of capital and lowercase letters. Select one handwriting style and stay with it, preferably the style in which you can write most quickly and legibly. Try to keep the size of your letters consistent.

Since you need to write quite a bit larger than you normally do, use your whole arm when you write. If you move only your wrist, as you do when writing at a desk, the letters will be too small. The larger the letter you want, the larger your arm movement should be. To make your letters bold and thick, hold the marker so the wide part of the tip touches the paper most of the time.

Even if your handwriting is poor, do not avoid using flip charts. A meeting record in poor handwriting is much better than no record at all. The goal is to have useful, not beautiful, newsprint sheets. For the same reason, write as quickly as you can. If you take too much time to write, you will defeat your larger purpose. A participative meeting should not drag on too long, or people will lose their motivation to participate.

---

[10]Available from University Associates, 8517 Production Avenue, San Diego, California 92121, phone (619) 578-5900.

Most people worry about their spelling when they write on newsprint. Even some of the best spellers have trouble in this situation, probably because the writing is large and they are pressured to write quickly and in front of others. There are several ways to handle poor spelling. One is to simply spell your best and expect a few misspelled words. Another is to state up front that you do not always spell well. Ask for help when you get to a problem word. A third way (especially if you misspell words frequently) is to have someone else—a better speller—record for you.

A second principle of newsprint construction is to enhance your work with color or simple graphics whenever possible. Select colors that will make the newsprint useful and easy to read. The best colors for the main text are black, dark blue, and green, which show up the best from a distance. However, dark purple is also a readable color. Use red, orange, yellow, and other lighter colors for highlighting only. You can use this second color to write a few key words so they will stand out, to underline key phrases or words, to make "bullets," or to make the title stand out. A caution: Avoid using more than three colors on a page. Brandt (1986, p. 40) has this suggestion: "Two colors are better than one. Three aren't bad if done carefully and with purpose. More than three tend to be a bit much. The audience may have difficulty picking up accents or emphasis."

A graphic or picture always gets attention. Use graphics, however, not only to get attention but also for a purpose: to enhance, augment, or explain. Again, Brandt's book has a wealth of ideas for graphics, or use your own. Look through books on your topic or find art or children's books with simple pictures.

The third consideration when you prepare newsprint is spacing. As a general rule, write only seven to twelve lines on a newsprint sheet prepared in advance. For a sheet with a few key phrases that you will refer to again and again, five or six lines is better. When recording people's ideas during a meeting, however, you need to get more lines on a sheet—or you will use too many sheets and run out of room to post the ideas on walls. Some newsprint flip charts come with light-blue grid lines spaced an inch apart. Write letters an inch high and skip an inch between lines, so you have room for twelve to fifteen lines of writing per page.

The fourth principle is to post newsprint sheets during the meeting so they will be useful to the group. Some rooms do not have enough wall space or have walls that masking tape does not stick to. Masking tape is best for hanging newsprint, unless your meeting room has strips of cork that you can push pins into. Transparent tape damages paint and wallpaper.

HANDLING AND STORING NEWSPRINT

The quickest and most efficient way to post newsprint is to tear off small strips of inch-wide masking tape ahead of time and attach them to the easel that supports and displays the flip chart (see Figure 9). When you are ready to post a sheet, attach a piece of tape to the upper-left and upper-right sides of the paper before tearing the sheet off the flip chart. (Once the sheet has been torn off, you will have a hard time grabbing the tape, attaching it to the paper, and posting the sheet.) If you are short, ask someone who is taller to help you with posting.

Tearing the sheets off the flip-chart pad can be a problem. Some newsprint just does not tear well. On the other hand, some newsprint has perforated holes, and some easels allow for better tearing than others. One way to tear off a newsprint sheet is to hold down the pad with one hand firmly at the top (the left if you are right-handed, vice versa if you are left-handed) and grasp the sheet at the bottom with the other hand. Then pull down on the sheet, starting the tear at the perforations. The sheet will usually tear easily then. This method is similar to

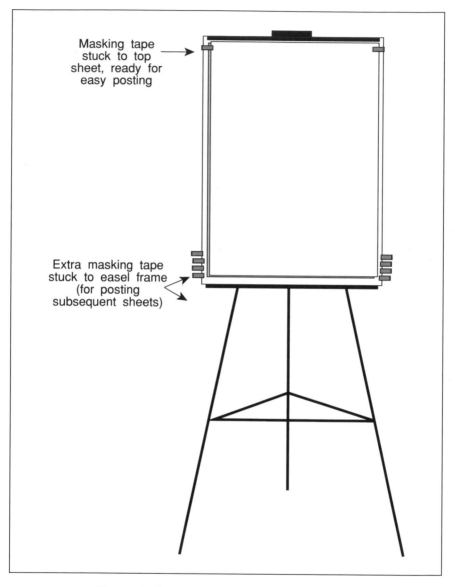

Masking tape stuck to top sheet, ready for easy posting

Extra masking tape stuck to easel frame (for posting subsequent sheets)

Figure 9. Preparing Newsprint for Posting

how you would tear a piece of paper off an ordinary writing pad.

If this does not work, use the "confidence method," which not only always works but will give you a sense of power. The number-one rule here is to approach the flip chart with confidence. Grasp the sheet at the bottom left corner with your right hand (if you are right-handed). Lift it up, gathering momentum as you go. Grab the top of the easel with your left hand, and rip the sheet off the pad with one smooth tearing motion. Your right hand will make a large arc to the right. The edges of the paper will be a bit uneven, but the rest of the chart will be intact.

Other ways of tearing off sheets have been discovered, and each person will find a way that works best for him or her. The only reason the subject is discussed here is to let you know that people often have trouble tearing sheets off flip charts, that continually ripping up the hard work of the group can be frustrating (and funny), and that with a little practice tearing can be easy and natural.

Filled newsprint sheets sometimes need to be stored for later transcription or for reuse at another meeting. Arrange the sheets in chronological order and number them. If possible, store them flat. If not, roll them up and secure them with a rubber band. Label the roll on the outside so the charts can be found easily. You may want to roll them so the printed pages face up; in this way, when they are opened at a later date, they will not roll upward and cover up the wording.

NEWSPRINT AS A MEETING RECORD

If the filled newsprint sheets are being transcribed as a meeting record, have the transcriber copy the exact wording and order of the sheets. People can recall the work of the meeting better if the sheets are not reorganized, cleaned up, and reworded. Editing the sheets may cause a group to struggle for quite some time to recapture what it did.

Newsprint sheets of information are an important part of the team's work. They serve as a working document during the meeting and an important record of the group's work and decisions, which can be transcribed or left as is for future reference.

11

Managing the Group Process

STRUCTURE WITHOUT STRANGULATION

Productive meetings need adequate time for participation with enough structure to keep them on track and on schedule. Participation alone is not necessarily productive. Meetings that go on much longer than planned or that veer off the targeted schedule tend to be unproductive. Participants begin to fidget, wondering when the meeting will adjourn or when it will move on. Even highly interactive meetings need limits on time and topics to avoid wasting valuable time and energy on unrelated issues.

The facilitator's role is to balance open participation with structure. When the group strays too far, refer to the objectives of the meeting. Say something like "This subject is interesting and certainly important, but it isn't getting us any closer to our objective for today. Let's go back to...." If the group members forget the process, remind them of what they are supposed to be doing: "Remember, we're just brainstorming now. We'll evaluate and discuss each idea later." It is also appropriate to ask a speaker how his or her point relates to the issue or objective: "Will you explain to us how your point relates to...?" or "The points you're making are important, but they're not helping us accomplish our objective."

SUMMARIZING AND BRIDGING

From time to time, the facilitator should stop and *summarize* what has been said to refocus the group on its objective. Completed newsprint sheets are a good tool for summarizing. Look back at the newsprint with the group and highlight what has occurred so far. Say something like "We've heard a lot of good thoughts. Let me see if I can summarize where we are now" or "We're getting away from our objective. Let's summarize and move on."

Let someone in the group summarize whenever possible: "Where are we at this point? Will someone please summarize what we have said so far?" The group then has the opportunity to reflect on both the content and the process of the meeting. But be prepared to summarize when someone else cannot. Some facilitators take a few notes during the discussion to help them summarize later.

After summarizing, move on to the next question or activity. Do not allow people to begin discussing ground that has already been covered, unless the group insists on doing so. You may be able to "read the group" and determine that moving on would be counterproductive. You must then come up with a process that will allow the group to complete its work on the old subject. One technique is to say "We seem to need to discuss this some more. What is it we haven't covered?" Perhaps a topic needs to be dealt with separately, at another meeting. If so, record the topic on newsprint and make it one of the action items for the next meeting. If the topic needs to be addressed before moving on, take time to discuss it fully and reach some kind of consensus. Otherwise, it may come up again and again throughout the meeting.

Another way to keep the group on track is to *bridge* from one activity or topic to another. Bridging consists of first summarizing the previous work and then explaining to the group what is going to happen next and how it relates to the previous work and to the meeting objective. For example: "We've listed several possible causes of the problem. Now let's take a different look at the problem by listing who and what could be benefiting from it." (The facilitator then begins a newsprint sheet with the heading "Who/What May Be Benefiting from the Problem.") Another sort of bridge is a short break before the next activity.

Bridging can take place during a discussion as well. Point out how one person's comment relates to another's to provide a kind of "glue" holding together a lot of different points: "I think that supports what Ann said earlier" or "Does that address one of your earlier concerns, Dave?"

Although structure is important, it is a good idea to avoid too tight a structure. People need time to think, discuss, wander off the topic a little, and be creative. A certain amount of wandering can be productive. Side issues that relate to the main issue can be touched on. People can "vent" frustrations, and the facilitator can acknowledge the validity of those frustrations. These little "side trips" often bring out important data, giving the facilitator insights into people's perspectives and related concerns. These wanderings, however, should not dominate the meeting.

MIRRORING

A technique called *mirroring* allows the facilitator to help the group monitor itself. From time to time, the facilitator comments on either the content or the process of the meeting and then asks the group to respond. For example, the facilitator may mention that the group is commenting only on the disadvantages of a particular alternative. This observation then focuses the group on the *content* of its work. Or the facilitator might observe that, whenever someone brings up a radically different viewpoint, the rest of the group ignores that person. This observation focuses the group members on how they are working together, the *process* of the meeting. The facilitator may also mirror a ground rule that the group is violating: "Even though we agreed to hear everyone out, there's a lot of interrupting going on. How does this affect the team?" A comment like this encourages the group to adhere to its own norms and to change behaviors when those norms are violated.

Another way to mirror is to ask team members to comment on how the team is progressing, how well it is functioning, or how well it has met its objectives and expectations. The facilitator can ask for volunteers to comment or can ask each person separately to ensure that everyone is heard from. Encouraging team members to evaluate the team's progress from time to time fosters teamwork. It reinforces the idea that everyone has responsibility for the work of the team and that everyone's comments are worth listening to.

GETTING THE GROUP UNSTUCK

Groups frequently get bogged down, become confused, or have trouble letting go of an issue. The facilitator can use several techniques to move a group forward when it gets stuck. If the group gets bogged down in specifics, move on to generalities: "We seem to be stuck on detail. Can someone give us the 'big picture' of what we're talking about?" When the group members are stuck on generalities, move them to specifics: "I'm hearing a lot of generalities; can someone give us some specifics?"

The group may get stuck on an issue that does not relate directly to the objectives. If this happens, tell the group you would like to stop for a few minutes and record the key points of this issue on a sheet of newsprint. Mention that this may be something the group will decide to work on another time. Then ask the group to come back to the objectives and issue at hand.

One maxim that holds true for meetings and group work is "If people can get confused, they will." Their confusion is not necessarily a negative or bad thing—just a fact. Words can be interpreted differently, people have different perspectives, and any topic generally offers more information than people can deal with at one time. One of the facilitator's responsibilities, then, is to recognize confusion and help the group through it. Meetings can also be designed to minimize typical sources of confusion.

How should confusion be handled? First, acknowledge it. When appropriate, gently but firmly state that the group seems to be confused and that it needs to take time out to clear up the confusion. Second, mirror to the group what you are hearing. Third, try to sort out what the group is confused about. Use the newsprint to draw a model or to number and list the confusing points; do whatever you can to explain the confusion. Check with the group members to see if you have understood the problem. They may understand it better than you do. Then ask, "What can we do to clear this up and move on?" Or suggest a process that will help the group move on. For example, you may suggest saving some parts of the discussion for later in the process. You may refer to the topic that the confusion is about and clarify what was decided earlier. You may need to write something out for the whole group to see and then check to see if everyone agrees on it. The solution depends, of course, on the situation. The key is to recognize and clear up the confusion so the group can proceed.

USING SUBGROUPS TO GET THINGS DONE

Research has shown that the most productive group consists of five to nine members and that an odd number of people is better than an even number. With an odd number, tie votes and splits down the middle can be avoided. A facilitator with a group of more than nine people should consider breaking it down into smaller units from time to time to accomplish specific tasks.

Here are some circumstances that lend themselves to breaking a group into smaller units:

- When the task requires special expertise and not all members have that expertise;

- When there is too much work and dividing the work will increase efficiency;

- When you want to encourage certain people to work together—for example, to discourage cliques, to put together people who are highly motivated to work together, to give everyone a chance to work closely with everyone else, to allow one person's expertise to complement others', to have a more experienced or skilled person coach others;

- When you want to give people a chance to choose which part of a project they want to work on; and

- When you want different groups to work on the same task, perhaps to foster more creativity, to generate several viable alternatives, or to increase everyone's learning and involvement.

Whenever possible, let people form their own subgroups. Make certain each subgroup clearly understands its particular objective.

Even if you use subgroups, you should keep the larger group intact for some of the work. In particular, bring the subgroups back together frequently for discussion, review, and final decisions. If you do not, you may end up with several smaller teams instead of one large team.

"READING" THE GROUP AND MAKING ADJUSTMENTS

The facilitator's ability to read the group accurately is a critical and invaluable skill. Meetings generally do not run smoothly. Even with careful planning, people may be sidetracked to a more volatile issue or the process may not go very well. Facilitators need to be able to recognize these problems and adjust. A productive meeting is not always a highly controlled one. The more participation there is, the more difficult it is to predict people's needs and responses—and the more difficult it is to conduct a meeting exactly as planned.

Reading the group during a meeting requires attentiveness to what is going on for individuals as well as for the group as a whole. A skilled facilitator pays attention to both the verbal and nonverbal behaviors of the participants.

People signal their feelings through eye contact, posture, voice tone and volume, and facial expression. Their nonverbal clues may indicate:

- Enthusiasm and high energy level;
- Inattention (doing other things);
- Boredom or discomfort (yawning, looking away, reading);
- Confusion;
- Anger, disdain, exasperation, and so on (rolling the eyes);
- Nervousness; and
- Agreement or satisfaction (nodding and smiling).

Verbal behaviors also offer important clues. Observe who is participating and how much. What is the conversation centering on? What is not being talked about? Is there a balance between facts and feelings? Is there general clarity or confusion? Is the leader in the background or foreground? Is leadership being shared among the group, or is one person clearly the leader? Are individual members hindering or helping the group's progress?

If most of the group members seem interested and involved, the meeting is probably going well. Some healthy disagreement usually means people are being open about their thoughts and feelings. However, a low energy level, apathy, or boredom may indicate that the group needs a change of pace. You can revitalize the group with a short break, a new activity, a different process, a change to subgroups, a new topic, or even adjournment and continuation of the meeting at a later time.

Frequently you will know that something is wrong but not know what it is. When this happens, ask the group, "What's happening right now for people?" or "We've lost much of our energy; what do we need to do now?" When the group has too much energy and is becoming unruly, you might say, "There's a lot of energy on this topic, but we're losing our productivity. Let's discuss one point at a time."

Sometimes groups focus too much on either the facts or the feelings connected with a topic. When this happens, try suggesting that the group think about the topic from another angle. For example, if the group is expressing a lot of strong feelings without many facts, intervene and say, "We've aired a lot of feelings on this issue, and this is good. Let's bring out some of the facts." If the group is putting forth facts but avoiding the feelings associated with an issue, steer the group by saying, "We've covered many facts related to this issue. What are some of your feelings about what we are discussing?"

An imbalance of participation is another problem. You can restore balance by seeking the opinions of quieter individuals: "Jane, we haven't heard from you on this issue. What are some of your thoughts?" If one side of the room is quieter than the other or one subgroup is not participating, ask for some input from that group: "I'd like to hear from...."

Just remember that the facilitator's role is to guide the process, leading the group so it accomplishes its work. If the meeting process needs to be adjusted to make this happen, then the facilitator must either make adjustments or accept the suggestions of meeting participants, who sometimes have better ideas about what will work. The facilitator is not divine; he or she cannot lay out a perfect meeting each time. It is more likely that the facilitator will need to navigate the meeting, turning when needed to make participation productive.

HANDLING DIFFICULT INDIVIDUALS

From time to time, any member of a group may become difficult. A well-focused and well-facilitated meeting can overcome most difficult situations, but some will always remain.

Facilitators can follow some general rules when a difficult situation arises. First, handle the problem before it gets out of hand. Second, do not embarrass people, because "embarrassed kittens become tigers." Third, protect everyone's self-esteem throughout any difficult situation. And fourth, take control in a firm, positive, constructive way.

How do you know when to intervene? A good rule of thumb is to ask yourself whether the group's productivity and enjoyment are being affected. If the answer is "yes," then it is time to do something.

When someone is hurting the productivity of the group, you have three choices: to deal with this person in front of the group, during a break, or not at all. For the sake of productivity, the last choice is probably not a good one. Sometimes the problem goes away without any intervention, but if it does not, the facilitator will eventually need to do something.

When you can constructively and positively handle the situation in front of the group, do so to maintain productivity. Here are some suggestions:

- "Matt, you've made several fine points today. Now I would like to hear comments from someone else."
- "Kathy, you made that point earlier. See, it's recorded on newsprint."
- "Jim, is there something you and Bill would like to share with the rest of the group?" or "Jim and Bill, I'd like to have only one meeting at a time." Move toward those engaged in the side conversation, and then wait until they stop.
- "Sue, it seems that you don't agree we should take this approach. Why? What would you like to see happen?" This technique gives the person a chance to vent feelings and gives others a chance to address the person's concerns.
- Ask a withdrawn, overly quiet person to help you.

If you cannot resolve the problem gracefully in front of the entire group, wait until break time to discuss the problem with the individual. You might want to speak to a perpetual latecomer at the break. Or if one group member has been vociferously opposing someone else's idea, you can say something like "Sue, you seem to take issue with Mary every time she addresses XYZ. After the break, would you be willing to give us some of your ideas about how you would rather proceed?"

Several types of people often create problems during meetings. The *overly talkative* person who comments too frequently is one of them. Others get discouraged or frustrated waiting for him or her to finish, and the group loses the benefit of other viewpoints. This person may be a show-off or a windbag. He or she may also be exceptionally well informed and eager to contribute. Regardless, when this person dominates the meeting, the group's energy level will go down, and others will withdraw. Sometimes the group members will correct this type of person, but when they do not, the facilitator must intervene to maintain productivity. As the facilitator, you can cut across this person's talk with a summarizing statement and a direct question to someone else—for example: "That's an interesting point; now let's hear from Jennifer."

Another kind of person who poses a problem is the one who *rambles*—who talks about things other than the subject, uses farfetched analogies, or gets lost before reaching the point. When a rambler stops for breath, thank him or her, refocus attention by restating the relevant points and reminding the group of its objective, and move on. You may indicate, "We need to get back to our subject."

Other people may be *inarticulate*. They have contributions to make but lack the ability to put those contributions into the proper words. You can help out by listening and then restating the person's ideas: "Let me repeat that." Help such a person express his or her ideas so they make sense to the group.

A different problem occurs when someone just *will not talk*. Try to determine what is motivating the person, whether boredom, indifference, timidity, or feelings of superiority or insecurity. Is the person new to the group or from a culture that believes it is rude to jump in or interrupt someone else? Your action will depend on the motivation. Seek suitable ways to involve the person. Ask direct questions that you are sure the person can answer. Ask for his or her agreement or opinion on views expressed by others.

When someone is definitely wrong and continues to come up with obviously incorrect comments, the group will become annoyed. Wrong information also gets in the way of productivity. This situation must be handled delicately. As a facilitator, you can intervene with "I can see how you feel," "That's one way of looking at it," or "I see your point, but can we reconcile that with the true situation?" An even more direct approach would be to ask "What are some facts to support what you are saying?"

The *obstinate* individual is one who just will not budge. He or she does not see the point and will not go along with the rest of the group. Try to get the others to help this person see their point of view. When you are ready to move on, say something like "I'm sure you have a reason for your point of view, but I'd like you to try to consider the group's viewpoint for now."

The *latecomer* is perpetually late to group meetings or darts in and out of meetings to carry on other business. Avoid confronting the person in front of the group. Wait until during a break or after the meeting. Find out why the person is always late (there may be an important reason). Point out why this behavior is disruptive, and ask the latecomer to help you figure out a solution. When the latecomer arrives, ask someone else to quickly review what is going on, and then continue.

Similar to the latecomer is the *early leaver*. A person who leaves before the meeting ends drains the energy of the group and misses the most important part of the meeting, which is getting to consensus and closure. At the beginning of the meeting, check to see if everyone can stay until the end. If all participants commit to staying until the end of the meeting, a potential early leaver is less likely to sneak out. If you do not need everyone until the end, tell the group ahead of time. Also, check to see that your meetings keep to the scheduled time, are not too unstructured or boring, and involve everyone in the group.

12

Getting to Consensus
and Closure

WHAT CONSENSUS IS AND IS NOT

Consensus is a point of maximum agreement so action can follow. According to Doyle and Straus (1976), it is a win-win solution, in which "everyone feels that he or she has won...a solution that does not compromise any strong convictions or needs" (p. 56).[11] Consensus is not achieved by voting, by imposing a win-lose outcome, by dictating the conclusion, or by people's abdicating or giving in. To reach consensus, group members share ideas, discuss and evaluate, debate, organize and prioritize ideas, and struggle to reach the best conclusion together. Reaching consensus is the act of gaining general agreement. A good test for consensus is to ask the question "Can you support this decision?" If everyone can support it, the group has achieved 100-percent consensus.

---

[11] From *How to Make Meetings Work* by M. Doyle and D. Straus, 1976, New York: Jove Books. Reprinted by permission.

WHEN TO USE CONSENSUS

Consensus is not always the best strategy. In some cases, reaching consensus does not result in a better decision or outcome. Group members are capable of unanimously agreeing on a completely incorrect solution to a problem. On certain occasions, however, consensus remains a highly desirable goal. When a group must make an important decision that requires the commitment of all members, consensus is the best approach.

The process of reaching a consensus takes time and should not be rushed. The process works best when it has been carefully planned, when the instructions are clear, and when the facilitator is skilled in using such leadership techniques as brainstorming and problem labeling. Studies have shown that groups using a systematic, rational method to make decisions and solve problems make higher-quality decisions than groups that do not proceed rationally. The facilitator plays a critical role in seeing that the group uses a rational method and a structured process.

Because it takes time and skill, consensus should be reserved for important decisions requiring a high degree of support and commitment from those who will implement the decisions.

HOW TO MAKE CONSENSUS WORK

To make consensus work, the leader must become skilled at separating the content of the team's work (the task itself) from the process (how the team goes about doing the task). But the process is what needs the most attention.

Gordon (1977) emphasizes this point:

> An effective group leader...does not need to *solve* problems, but to *see to it that they get solved*. Instead of being a good problem-solver, the effective leader must be a good *facilitator of problem-solving*. Central to this conception of

leader effectiveness is the requirement that the leader understands that problem-solving is a *process* and that he or she must learn certain skills that will get that process started and take it to a successful completion. (p. 47)[12]

One of the facilitative leader's key responsibilities is to help others solve their own problems. The leader who wants his or her team members to become skilled at problem solving will teach them a process for solving problems, without solving the problems for them.

THE PROBLEM-SOLVING PROCESS

The problem-solving process involves the following steps, each of which requires group participation:

1. Identify the problem or goal.
2. Generate alternative solutions.
3. Establish objective criteria.
4. Decide on a solution that best fits the criteria.
5. Proceed with the solution.
6. Evaluate the solution.

A meeting should be structured so everyone knows exactly which step is being worked on at any point.

Discussion and creative thinking are more likely to occur when the steps are introduced with open questions like the following:

1. *Identify the problem or goal.* Problem: What is the problem? How do you see the problem? What seems to be causing the problem? If the problem were solved,

---

[12] From *Leader Effectiveness Training (L.E.T.): The No-Lose Way to Release the Productive Potential of People* by T. Gordon, 1977, Ridgefield, CT: Wyden. Reprinted by permission.

what would happen? Goal: What are we trying to achieve? Where do we want to end up?

2. *Generate alternative solutions.* What are possible solutions? If we had no restraints, what would we do to solve the problem?

3. *Establish objective criteria.* What objective and measurable criteria must the solution meet?

4. *Decide on the alternative that best fits the criteria.* How well does each alternative meet our criteria? Which solution best fits the criteria? Is this the best decision?

5. *Implement the decision.* Who needs to do what and by when?

6. *Evaluate the solution.* How well did the solution solve the problem?

A skilled facilitator can use other group processes to help achieve consensus. Remember when using any of the following techniques to keep the L.E.A.D. model in mind. First, explain the purpose of each process to the group. Second, motivate group members to become meaningfully involved. Third, aim for—but do not rush—consensus. Allow time for meandering, disagreement, and discussion. Move the group members to consensus by asking "Do we have general agreement on this point?" When the members do not agree, allow time for more discussion. At some point agreement may become necessary. You can move the group toward action by stating "Even though we have differences of opinion on this point, we do agree on.... I suggest that now we move forward so we can achieve our objective."

IDENTIFYING THE PROBLEM

When people sense a problem, they are usually reacting to problem symptoms. Something is happening that should not be happening, or something should be but is not happening. But such symptoms are side effects of the real problem, which usually lies beneath the surface. The leader's role is to guide the group in identifying the real problem or the various parts of the real problem (problems in organizations tend to be complex). Questioning and labeling are two techniques the leader can use to involve the group in problem identification.

Questioning

Much can be discovered about a problem and its root cause through the simple process of asking questions. The point is to understand the whole problem before rushing to solve what may be only a symptom of the problem. By answering questions, people get a broader understanding of the problem and avoid jumping to premature conclusions.

Begin by asking these two questions: "What is happening that should not be? What should be happening that is not?" Record each group member's input and then post the list. The next step is to involve the group in asking and answering a series of questions together. Use a newsprint sheet on which you have printed the words "Who," "What," "When," and "Where." Ask the group to identify *who* is involved with the problem; *what* materials, processes, equipment, and so forth are involved with the problem; *when* the problem occurs; and *where* the problem occurs. Record each input as you go, and then ask the flip side of the who/what/when/where questions: "Who is *not* involved with the problem?" "What materials, processes, equipment, and so on are *not* involved with the problem?"

Here are some additional questions you can ask the group to answer:

- "How do you see what is going on?"
- "How does the problem affect you?"
- "What is likely to happen if the problem is not addressed and resolved?"

- "What are likely causes of the problem?"
- "What seems to be the real problem?"
- "What seems to be the root cause of the problem?"
- "What are the key benefits of solving the problem?"

Continue asking questions until you begin to get the same answers over and over again. Then ask the group members if they feel the need to gather more data before going on to the next step. If they do, assign responsibilities for gathering the data, and plan to deal with the problem at the next meeting. But once the group has sufficient data, you can move on.

Labeling

The next step is labeling the problem in such a way that the group can focus on its solution. You have two ways to do this. The first is to state the problem in terms of what needs to happen and what is preventing it from happening. Here are some examples:

- "Our goal is to handle customer assignments on time and in a quality way, but our customers continually clamor to get their work assigned number-one priority with a due date of 'as soon as possible.'"
- "Lack of communication among the specialists in our department makes it difficult to provide service to our customers when someone is absent from the office."
- "Budgets are due on October 1, but it is September 20 and we still do not have the volume projections for next year."

The second way to label the problem is to state it in the form of a question:

- "How can we accomplish our goal of handling customer assignments on time and in a quality way when our customers continually clamor to get their work assigned number-one priority with a due date of 'as soon as possible'?"

- "How can we improve communication among the specialists in our department so customers can receive service when someone is absent from the office?"
- "How can we get the volume projections in time to get the budget in by October 1?"

GENERATING ALTERNATIVES

The most common way to generate alternatives is through brainstorming. After generating as many alternatives as possible with brainstorming, those ideas may be grouped into categories through the process of clustering. Later the clustered ideas can be dealt with in an organized manner.

Brainstorming

Most people are familiar with brainstorming, although few have experienced it in the way it works best. What is supposed to happen during a brainstorming session is that people think of as many ideas as possible—any idea is acceptable. The goal is to get as many ideas as possible to look at. Without a skilled facilitator, however, the brainstorming process frequently gets mixed up with the process of discussing and evaluating the ideas. People in the group say things like "That's an interesting idea. However, it won't work here because..." or "Yes, but what about the policy that forbids...?" This is not brainstorming in the classic sense.

If you allow the group to deviate from the correct process, you diminish the value of brainstorming. To facilitate a brainstorming session, you should therefore make sure the group follows these steps in order:

1. Give people a problem or a question to focus on.

2. Have each person write down privately as many ideas as he or she can think of, no matter how far-fetched, that might solve the problem or answer the question. (Sometimes the most far-fetched ideas inspire the best solution.)

3. Record and post all ideas without discussing or evaluating them.

4. Encourage people to build on one another's ideas and continue recording and posting all ideas.

5. Clarify the ideas. Give everyone a chance to look at the ideas and ask questions about the meaning of any idea. Do not evaluate any of the ideas at this time.

The following paragraphs present a more detailed look at each of the five steps:

1. *Give people a problem or a question to focus on.* To start the brainstorming session, post the key question to be addressed for all the group to see. If you have labeled a problem in the form of a question, you can use the label to focus the group. For example: "How can we improve communication among the specialists in our department so customers can receive service when someone is absent from the office?

2. *Have each person write down privately as many ideas as he or she can think of, no matter how far-fetched, that might solve the problem or answer the question.* It is important to allow time for people to think privately, because once the ideas begin to be posted, individuals may alter their own thinking. Emphasize that "any idea goes," and encourage people not to edit or censor their own ideas.

3. *Record and post all ideas without discussion or evaluation.* One approach that works well is to proceed around the room, person by person, and get one idea from everyone. Complete this process again and again until people have run out of ideas. Remember to capture the ideas accurately and to write down all new contributions. Tear off the filled newsprint sheets and post them for all to see. If someone's idea

sounds like one that has already been recorded, ask that person if his or her idea is the same. If so, do not record it again. If the person says it is different, post the idea. (When recording the ideas, you might want to number them; the numbers will help when you are referring to and grouping the ideas.) People will be tempted to ask for clarification or expansion of an idea or to comment on an idea. Disallow these types of comments, explaining that discussion and clarification will come later.

4. *Encourage people to build on one another's ideas and continue recording and posting all ideas.* Ask if anyone has any ideas that are new or that build on what someone else has suggested. Do not be surprised if you have several newsprint sheets filled with ideas at this point.

5. *Clarify the ideas.* After all ideas have been generated and recorded, give the group a chance to ask questions about them. The person who contributed the idea can be asked to comment on the intent or meaning of the idea. The group's goal is to clarify and understand each idea, not to evaluate it or discuss it in detail.

Clustering

Evaluating twenty to fifty ideas can be quite cumbersome. Clustering is grouping the ideas into categories to help organize the evaluation process. If only a few ideas are generated, this step is probably not necessary. However, brainstorming usually generates a long list of ideas, many of which relate to other ideas.

The first step in clustering is to ask the group which ideas are related. Use letters or different colored markers to indicate which ideas can be grouped together for ease of discussion. Get general agreement here. If some group members prefer to keep an idea separate, honor their reasoning and move on. Some ideas will not lend themselves to clustering.

The second step is to label each idea group with an appropriate title. For example, all ideas relating to improving human relations could be grouped together under "Human Relations." Ideas relating to monetary resources and budget could be called "Money" or "Budget." Make a list of the categories somewhere, and list either the ideas themselves or the numbers of the ideas that go into each category.

The purpose of clustering is to organize ideas for further discussion and evaluation, so do not rewrite them. If nothing else, you will save time. If you adjourn the meeting and give someone the assignment of rewriting the ideas in clusters, caution him or her not to change any wording. No individual should be given the group's responsibility to weed out and refine the ideas.

ESTABLISHING CRITERIA

The next step in the problem-solving process is to get people to agree on what criteria they are going to use to evaluate the alternatives. Some argue that criteria should be established before brainstorming. Obviously, the brainstorming step influences the criteria step and vice versa. However, if criteria are established after brainstorming, the brainstorming process can be more creative and unrestrained. Another advantage is that the brainstorming process is likely to open people's minds to new ideas and help keep them from being rigid in the criteria-setting process.

There are two types of criteria: (1) essential criteria, which solutions must meet, and (2) desirable criteria, which it would be nice to meet. Ask the group to classify the criteria as either essential or desirable.

Also make sure that each criterion is objective and measurable. Instead of specifying that something be affordable, for example, identify what "affordable" is. An essential criterion might be a solution that costs less than $100,000. Setting measurable criteria will ease the process of reaching consensus.

EVALUATING ALTERNATIVES

Any alternatives that do not meet the essential criteria can be eliminated. Those that remain can be evaluated on how well they meet the desirable criteria.

Sometimes a worthy idea is eliminated because it does not fit the essential criteria. You may want to suggest that the group consider changing such an idea to meet the essential criteria.

One or more solutions may fit both the essential and desirable criteria. At this stage the group members must come to a consensus about which solution best fits the criteria. They may decide that more than one solution must be implemented to solve the problem.

IMPLEMENTING THE DECISION

The next step is to break down the best alternative into manageable tasks, things that must be done to put the decision into effect. The question is "Who needs to do what and by when?"

First, have people in the group think of anything that must be done to implement the decision. Try to list things that can be done by one person, so responsibilities can be assigned. Second, number all the tasks; then indicate beside each task which others must be completed before that particular task can be started. Third, estimate the amount of time it will take to complete each task. Last, plot the tasks on a chart with a time line to help the group implement its decision on schedule.

EVALUATING THE SOLUTION

One of the most important things a leader-facilitator can do to develop a mature team is to get it to evaluate its own progress. When a problem has been solved and the solution has been implemented, have the team evaluate how well the solution solved the problem. What still needs to be addressed? Team members should also evaluate progress toward individual goals (the tasks), as well as their progress in working together. At first, the facilitator should build time for evaluation into the group meetings. Later, as the team matures, members will undoubtedly initiate their own evaluation.

Here are some questions to use in evaluating the results of a task and how well people worked together:

1. What went well as far as the task is concerned?
2. What should we do differently next time as far as the task is concerned?
3. What went well as far as the team's working together is concerned?
4. How shall we work together differently next time?

If the group is large, divide it into two subgroups. Have one subgroup answer questions 1 and 2 and the other subgroup answer questions 3 and 4. Then have each subgroup report its findings to the rest of the team.

KEEPING PEOPLE ON TRACK

When a group is involved in a problem-solving session, the facilitator is responsible for keeping the group members on track. To begin with, the facilitator must give clear directions about how to carry out each step. He or she will also need to steer people back to the topic when they wander. People's minds do not always work in an orderly fashion. For example, during the brainstorming process, people will naturally want to discuss the ideas as they are generated instead of waiting until later. Or when the group is establishing criteria, people are likely to begin discussing their advantages and disadvantages. In either case, the facilitator will need to intervene.

The group processes suggested here are only a few basic ones. The literature on group decision making, problem solving, and communication suggests many more techniques for bringing groups to consensus or helping them work together more productively. Some are more difficult to implement than others. Leader-facilitators must practice to find the ones they and their group are most comfortable with.

GETTING TO CLOSURE

At several points in the problem-solving process, consensus must be reached before the next step begins. At each juncture, the facilitator should state what the group has agreed on and then check with the group to make sure the statement is accurate. The best way to make sure everyone has agreed to the same thing is to write out what was decided and post it for all to see. If action planning is part of the group's work, for example, list the actions that must be performed, those who will undertake the actions, and the deadlines for completing them.

Documenting agreements for all to see serves several purposes:

- Clarifies what people are agreeing to;
- Provides a record of what was decided;
- Motivates people to keep their agreements (their names appear publicly beside assignments);

- Brings absent members accurately up to date; and
- Focuses attention and energy on the actions that must be carried out.

OTHER USEFUL TECHNIQUES

Other useful techniques include prioritizing and four-box analysis.

Prioritizing

A group frequently has too many issues at hand, too many problems that need to be addressed, or too many goals to deal with all at once. When such is the case, prioritizing will help. The first step is to compile a list of what needs addressing and label each item in sequence with a letter of the alphabet. Then open up a discussion by saying "Which of these should have the highest priority for our team now?" After group members have had a chance to think about and discuss the question, ask them to pick the three items (or four or five, whichever seems appropriate) that they think deserve the highest priority. Ask each member to write the letters of these items on a 3" x 5" card that you distribute.

To compile the results, you can have each person put one mark on a newsprint sheet beside the items he or she chose or collect the cards and tally the results during a break. Have the members work as a group to pick the three to five items that received the most votes. Then ask people to comment on their own selections. Once the top items have been discussed, ask whether anyone wants to change his or her vote. Once this final voting is finished, pick the top three to five vote getters and ask, "Can everyone support (name the items) as our highest priority?" Write these items on a separate newsprint sheet as a record of the group's decision.

An alternative is to have each person assign points to his or her own top items. Give each person a total of ten points to distribute, with the most points for the highest-priority choice and the least points for the lowest-priority choice. (The facilitator can decide whether to allow people to assign zeroes.) Here are some examples:

First person:	C	7 points
	F	2 points
	G	1 point
Second person:	A	2 points
	R	8 points
	M	0 points

Tally the points for each lettered item. The ones with the highest numbers of points are the highest-priority items.

Four-Box Analysis

When a group is struggling through a difficult period, four-box analysis is a method it can use to regain direction and a sense of purpose. This technique allows the team members to deal with any aspect of their work together, to recognize strengths they may have been overlooking, and to pinpoint areas for improvement. The team must answer four questions:

1. What is not going well and is flexible (can change)?
2. What is not going well and is firm (not likely to change or not within the group's power to change)?
3. What is going well and is flexible (can change)?
4. What is going well and is firm (not likely to change or not within the group's power to change)?

Figure 10 shows how these questions structure a four-box diagram. Responses to question 1 are those things that

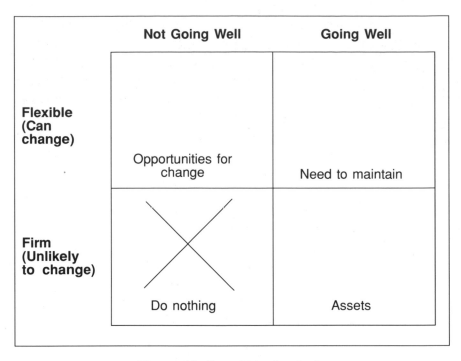

Figure 10. Four-Box Analysis

present the greatest opportunities for change. They are not going well, yet there is the potential for change. Responses to question 2 are things that are not going well but are out of the group's control. They are things about which the group can do nothing, so spending time and energy on them is unproductive. Responses to question 3 are things that are going well but, because they could change, need to be maintained. The group should continue to pay attention to these things and not take them for granted. Responses to question 4 represent those things the group can count on. They are going well and are not likely to change. These are the group's assets.

Once group members have collectively answered these questions and looked at their responses, they can focus on "opportunities for change." These are the things that need the attention of the group. The facilitator can suggest prioritizing them or using some other means to decide where to begin.

A group that has been struggling for some time should probably pick one thing to focus on at a time. It might also pick something that will be easy and quick to change, so it can feel successful right away. Starting with a difficult item may discourage the group even further.

FOLLOW-UP

Once team members agree on a plan of action, they must continue getting together to keep track of their progress. If too much time passes between meetings, team members may lose their motivation and deadlines may go by unnoticed.

Follow-up meetings do not need to be long. They can be a few minutes in length. But it is important for team members to come together to ensure that their decisions are being implemented and their problems are being solved. (They do not have to go through the whole process of decision making and problem solving again.) Without timely follow-up to the work that has been done, the team will be less motivated to work hard on the next problem. And if no time is set aside for follow-up, a question arises: Should time have been spent on the problem in the first place?

This question brings us full circle. A meeting must have a clear objective, and that objective must be worth the time required not only for meeting but also for following up. Two of the most common errors that leaders make are (1) holding meetings without clear, published objectives and (2) failing to follow up on the work done at those meetings. Meetings are a waste of time if nothing valuable gets accomplished or if the valuable work that is done goes nowhere.

A truly facilitative leader views meetings as a primary means of getting people to work together and puts time and effort into planning and leading meetings. The techniques and processes outlined in this book are only the basic tools for drawing successfully on team members' skills, knowledge, and diversity. The tools are not ends in themselves, nor are they exclusive or even unique to this book. But they will help leaders face the tremendous challenges of managing in an ever-changing, uncertain, and demanding world.

References and Bibliography

Bradford, D.L., & Cohen, A.R. (1984). *Managing for excellence.* New York: Wiley.

Bradford, L.P. (1976). *Making meetings work: A guide for leaders and group members.* San Diego, CA: University Associates.

Brandt, R.C. (1986). *Flip charts: How to draw them and how to use them.* Richmond, VA: Brandt Management Group.

Daniels, W.R. (1986). *Group power I: A manager's guide to using task-force meetings.* San Diego, CA: University Associates.

Doyle, M., & Straus, D. (1976). *How to make meetings work.* New York: Jove Books.

Fisher, B.A. (1980). *Small group decision making* (2nd ed.). New York: McGraw-Hill.

Fisher, R., & Ury, W. (1981). *Getting to yes.* Middlesex, England: Penguin Books.

Fordyce, J.K., & Weil, R. (1979). *Managing with people.* Reading, MA: Addison-Wesley.

Gordon, T. (1977). *Leader effectiveness training (L.E.T.): The no-lose way to release the productive potential of people.* Ridgefield, CT: Wyden.

Jay, A. (1968). How to run a meeting. *Harvard Business Review,* July-August.

Kimball, E.K. (1980). *How to get the most out of being a volunteer.* Phoenix, AZ: Jordan Press.

Mosvick, R.K., & Nelson, R.B. (1987). *We've got to start meeting like this!* Glenview, IL: Scott, Foresman.

Peck, M.S. (1978). *The road less traveled.* New York: Simon & Schuster.

Peoples, D.A. (1988). *Presentations plus: David Peoples' proven techniques.* New York: Wiley.

Pfeiffer, J.W., & Ballew, A.C. (1988). *Presentation and evaluation skills in human resource development.* San Diego, CA: University Associates.

Pokras, S. (1989). *Systematic problem-solving and decision-making.* Los Altos, CA: Crisp Publications.

Sayles, L.R. (1990, Spring). Leadership for the nineties: Challenge and change. *Issues & Observations,* pp. 8-11. Greensboro, NC: Center for Creative Leadership.

Schindler-Rainman, E., & Lippitt, R. (1975). *Taking your meetings out of the doldrums.* San Diego, CA: University Associates.

Index